THE RAILWAY EXECUTIVE
PASSENGERS
MUST NOT CROSS
THE LINE HERE

ODD CORNERS
OF THE
SOUTHERN

FROM THE DAYS OF STEAM

ODD CORNERS
OF THE
SOUTHERN

FROM THE DAYS OF STEAM

Alan Postlethwaite

SUTTON PUBLISHING

First published in the United Kingdom in 1999
Sutton Publishing Limited · Phoenix Mill · Thrupp · Stroud
Gloucestershire · GL5 2BU

British Library Cataloguing in Publication Data

A catalogue record for this book is available from the British Library.

ISBN 0-7509-1939-6

Endpapers: front: The staggered platforms, footbridge, barrow crossing, signal-box and station buildings at Wadhurst were elegantly laid out. Back: A gantry of LSWR low-pressure pneumatic signals at Basingstoke is flanked by two contrasting versions of Bulleid Pacific.

Frontispiece: The humble telegraph pole was a familiar feature of the steam railway. This short four-spar specimen is braced for a curve near Gomshall & Shere. It frames a Redhill-bound freight headed by a class N Mogul. Discarded sleepers are from the far track, recently re-laid with flat-bottom rail. The near track remains bullhead, the Southern standard until Nationalisation.

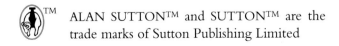 ALAN SUTTON™ and SUTTON™ are the trade marks of Sutton Publishing Limited

Typeset in Bembo 11/13pt.
Typesetting and origination by
Sutton Publishing Limited.
Printed in Great Britain by
Butler and Tanner, Frome, Somerset.

CONTENTS

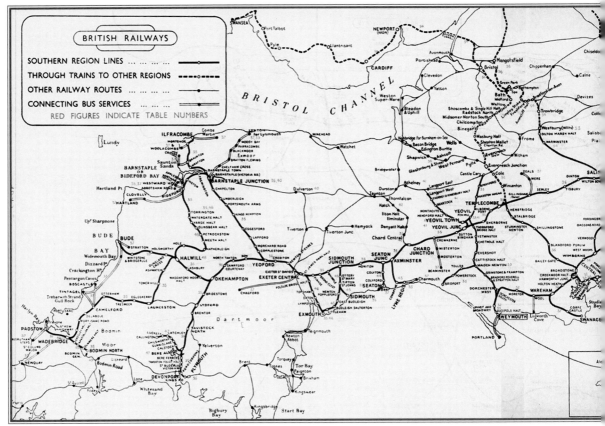

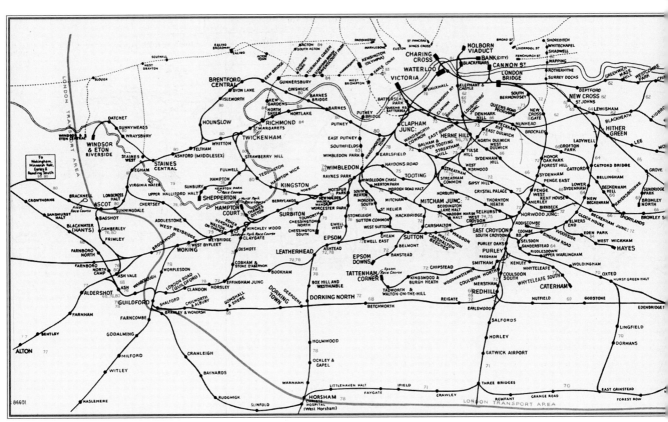

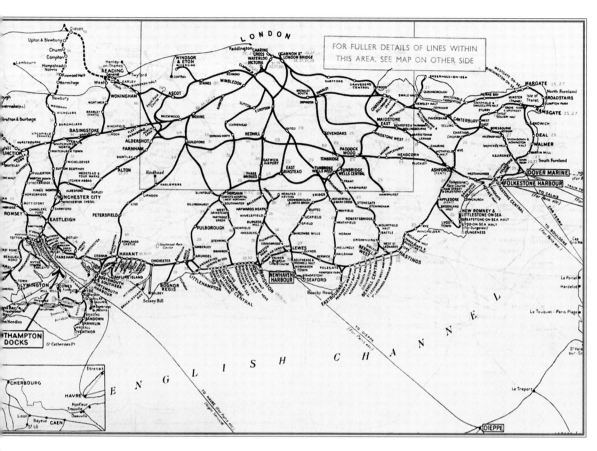

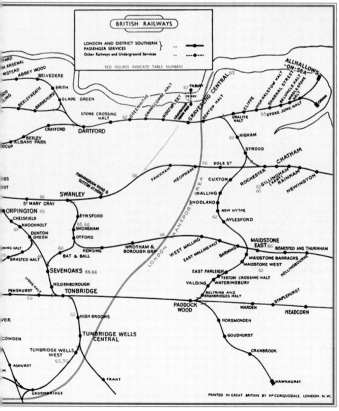

The elongated maps of BR(S) before the onset of the Beeching closures. A double-sided folded sheet measuring 27½ × 8½ in would be affixed to the rear of the Southern Region timetable, which was published twice a year and comprised over 1,000 pages. Similar maps were found in carriage compartments.

A composite picture at Oxted, featuring a pair of Sugg Rochester gas lamps on a 'barley-sugar' standard of LSWR/ SR design. The water crane is LBSCR, the signal-box is by Saxby & Farmer, the train is BR and the line is joint SER/ LBSCR. The signalman returns to his post after a short conversation with the driver of standard 2–6–4 tank No. 80032.

INTRODUCTION

The map of BR(S) – the Southern Region of British Railways – is elongated, covering the southern counties from Kent to Cornwall. Most of BR(S) was inherited from the Southern Railway (SR), one of the Big Four companies that were grouped by Parliament in 1923. The three principal pre-Group companies that made up the SR were:

The South Eastern & Chatham Railway (SECR), which served the coast from Margate to Hastings

The London, Brighton & South Coast Railway (LBSCR), which served from Hastings to Portsmouth

The London & South Western Railway (LSWR), which served from Portsmouth to Padstow

Inland, the lines of these companies converged and criss-crossed, particularly in the London area, often with intense rivalry and competition – the lines to Hastings and Portsmouth being prime examples. The LBSCR and LSWR were early companies, dating from the 1830s and '40s. The SECR, however, was a more recent name, formed in 1899 by the operational merger of two competitors to the Kent coast, namely the South Eastern Railway (SER), originating in the 1830s and '40s, and the London, Chatham & Dover Railway (LCDR), originating in the 1850s.

A batch of smaller railways were also part of the Southern grouping, including the following:

The Plymouth, Devonport & South Western Junction Railway (PD&SWJR)

The Isle of Wight Railway (IWR)

The Isle of Wight Central Railway (IWCR)

Finally to be represented in this book is the East Kent Railway (EKR), a colliery line that escaped the Grouping but was nationalised into BR(S) in 1948. The Southern Region of BR is therefore seen to be made up of at least ten earlier companies, each of which had strong individual characteristics and whose tangible assets endured the various mergers, groupings and Nationalisation. To visit the Southern during the years of BR steam was to discover a complex patchwork of buildings, signals, rolling stock, etc., covering an impressive span of ages, from the mid-nineteenth century to the mid-1960s. There were also many modified assets, which had been extended, improved, copied or relocated – hybrids and 'cuckoos in the nest' to challenge the intrepid railway archaeologist.

This book presents a view of BR(S) during the final decade of steam, identifying the characteristics and origins of stations, yards, signalling, signs, track, rolling stock, people, tickets, labels and notices. While many of the illustrations happen to incorporate steam, the focus is upon all the things that accompanied the steam age – subjects often inadequately described in the many excellent books on trains and locomotives. The eight thematic chapters illustrate, define and describe much of this 'other detail' for the benefit of historians, enthusiasts, preservationists and modellers. With this additional knowledge, one can attain the 'hi-fi' level of railway appreciation.

The illustrations were taken or collected by the author between 1958 and 1967. All are photographs except those in the final chapter, which are artefacts of paper or card – railway ephemera. Many of the photographs are what might be called 'composite' views, portraying several items of interest and thus relevant to more than one chapter. Cross-references are therefore given after the text of each chapter, intended to save time for the serious researcher. Other readers will doubtless prefer to browse the book at leisure and to unravel the different elements of these pictures for themselves. That is what steam railwaying was all about – having a day out, ostensibly with a particular purpose in mind, but in reality to 'browse' all the bits and pieces along the line, and to meet railway people in stations and odd corners. One was continually surprised by what turned up! To explore the railway was an enriching experience, and this book is intended to pass on for posterity some of those treasures, large and small, that largely disappeared with the end of steam and modernisation. Local freight also disappeared about this time and many branches were closed, increasing the historic interest of such illustrations.

One of the few overall roofs on the SR was at Callington, a terminus built by the PD&SWJR. Note the foreground lockbar, depressed by train wheels to prevent point operation. The ten-compartment third-class carriage is SECR, identified by its low elliptical roof, plain door ventilators and Z-shape hand rails.

Callington (*opposite*) is an example of the 'composite picture', comprising a station, a coach, a track feature, some barrows and seats. Such pictures are valuable not only for their wealth of detail but also for the overall 'atmosphere' of particular locations. Modellers in particular strive to create 'magic' layouts where the blend and positioning of buildings, sidings, signals, etc., looks 'just right'. This book offers such scenes; indeed, there is evidence to believe that the railway builders themselves often strove to produce combinations of beauty. The steam railway was more than a complex system ruled by mechanics, accounts and timetables. It was a work of art, an enduring asset to be proud of.

The author was brought up on the 'Southern Electric', so he did not enter railwaying through the usual route of observing locomotives and collecting numbers. Instead, he started as a modeller, progressing from clockwork Hornby tin-plate, through Hornby Dublo to Pecoway and 'Wonderful Wagons'. Upon leaving school, he started an engineering apprenticeship and attended evening classes in both engineering subjects and railway history, the latter almost by chance, in support of a friend whose father was in charge. For two winters, he attended Goldsmiths College in SE London, for evening lectures on railways, covering Britain as a whole and the Southern in particular. Field trips were made at weekends, and on one of these, in the New Cross area, he took an old box camera. For subsequent field trips to railway corners like Snow Hill, Herne Hill Sorting Sidings and Ashford, he borrowed a folding camera (2¼ in sq) and began to compose pictures with an element of artistry. Through this route, he discovered both the steam railway and the open countryside. This led to further evening classes in photography, the purchase of a 35 mm camera and numerous trips to all parts of the Southern and beyond. A better camera (with a fast shutter speed) was essential for moving trains, but most of the pictures in this book do not depict movement, so all three cameras are represented. The old box camera continues to hold its place!

Many of the detailed pictures were taken with modelling in mind. Cliffe, Hawkhurst, Brasted and Callington were mapped and photographed in fine detail – every sleeper was counted in the yard at Brasted. In the event, none of these was modelled by the author, but he still enjoys memories of the research. It is the market that determines ultimately which railway activities prevail, and the author's writing and photography have been appreciated far more than his modelling. He has nevertheless passed on to other modellers the fruits of his photography, thereby contributing to some fine 4 mm models, including ones of Axminster and Hawkhurst. Detailed photographs have also been passed on to preservationists researching their respective lines. This book is intended to help Southern modellers and researchers generally, as well as being a lively read for the average enthusiast.

Three years of the author's engineering apprenticeship were spent at Bankside Power Station, whose chimney-top afforded a panoramic view of the SECR's City approaches. From mid-afternoon, a succession of empty-stock steam trains, looking like z-gauge models, would wind their way slowly from Blackfriars via Metropolitan Junction to Cannon Street, ready for the evening exodus to the Kent coast. Bankside also introduced the author to a use of steam besides powering the locomotive – that of the generation of electricity. The principles are the same for both – fuel handling, combustion, ash and dust handling, steam raising, superheating, regulation through an expansion machine (turbine or cylinders), exhaust (to a condenser or atmosphere) and feed water preparation, storage and injection. Steam pressure is higher in power stations, and many refinements to improve performance are only possible when the plant does not have to be carried on wheels. The general public sees little or nothing of power plants – it is the preserve of a privileged few. What is more, power plants are aesthetically mundane and lack the fascination of travelling. They stand no comparison with the beautiful beasts that hauled the trains. And yet the engineering fascination and the principles remain the same, including the camaraderie, the pride of the workforce, the joy of playing with steam.

The wheels of progress roll on and it was the advent of electricity that started the decline of Southern steam. To compete with the electric tram, the LBSCR initiated its overhead electrification programme in the early 1900s. The LSWR followed suit, but using the outside-third rail system, which subsequently became the standard for the SR. But the greater threat to steam was the internal-combustion engine, both for road traffic and eventually on the railways. From the early 1920s, road traffic grew relentlessly, presenting a challenge to both passenger and freight rail services. The steam railway was unable to compete in terms of costs and comfort. Southern steam ended in 1967, yielding to electrification, dieselisation and the withdrawal of some services.

Enthusiasm for Southern steam has endured and grown, however, nurtured by the numerous preserved steam lines and museums and abetted by the many excellent books and journals. The Bluebell line was the pioneer of standard-gauge line preservation, opening in 1958 at its Sheffield Park end. Other preserved steam railways in the Southern area now include the Kent & East Sussex, the Sittingbourne & Kemsley, the Romney, Hythe & Dymchurch, the Spa Valley, the Isle of Wight, the Mid-Hants, the Swanage and the Bodmin & Wenford. Such enthusiasm extends not only to the locomotives and trains but to the architecture, accoutrements and way of life that went with them. Rightly or wrongly, it was a way of life that we now admire and yearn for. Preserved railways take trouble to dress their staff in the appropriate uniforms and to adorn their stations with authentic furniture and advertisements from the steam age. The Bluebell Railway, for example, installed a batch of replica LBSCR lamps and standards for their extension to East Grinstead. Such noble efforts ensure that we are still able to enjoy the atmosphere of the 'complete' steam railway.

General References

0.1 Dendy Marshal, C.F., revised by Kidner, R.W., *History of the Southern Railway*, Ian Allan, 1963.

0.2 St John Thomas, D., *A Regional History of the Railways of Great Britain*, Vol. 1, The West Country.

0.3 White, H.P., *A Regional History of the Railways of Great Britain*, Vol. 2, Southern England.

0.4 White, H.P., *A Regional History of the Railways of Great Britain*, Vol. 3, Greater London.

0.5 Davies, R., and Grant, M.D., *London and its Railways*, D&C, 1983.

0.6 St John Thomas, D., and Whitehouse, P., *SR 150, The Southern Railway*, Guild Publishing, 1988.

0.7 Whitehouse, P., and St John Thomas, D., *The Great Days of the Southern Railway*, BCA, 1992.

0.8 Paye, P., *Isle of Wight Railways Remembered*, OPC, 1984.

0.9 Kichenside, G.M., *Isle of Wight Album*, Ian Allan, 1967.

0.10 Allen, C.J., *Salute to the Southern*, Ian Allan, 1974.

Chapter One

PASSENGER STATIONS

Reference 0.1 lists around 1,085 SR stations, including 230 closed ones. The simplest stations were 'occupational' halts used by workmen at railway yards and lineside industries. They were unmanned and comprised little more than a platform, a rear fence and perhaps a couple of lamps. Next was the unmanned public halt, which had road access, a basic shelter, a nameboard and a board with train times. Nowadays, it might also incorporate a huge car park but in the days of steam, people walked to the railway. Two such halts are illustrated – Yarde and Chilsworthy – having different materials of construction and with respective platform lengths of one and two-and-a-bit coaches. Such single-line halts could be quaint and pleasant in summer but eerie and bleak in winter, especially at night. Tickets were bought from the guard. Langston also looked like a halt but it did in fact have a small booking office that was staffed intermittently.

Proper stations were manned continually, with better waiting facilities and heating, altogether rather more welcoming to the traveller. Although single-storey and plain-rectangular, the brick building at Mill Hill is an example of a basic but comfortable station. Basic stations could also be found on the elevated urban lines, generally lacking sidings, toilets and architectural merit. Examples are Brixton, South Bermondsey and Ludgate Hill – functional mass people-movers for commuting to the Metropolis.

More numerous and more pleasing to the eye were the small country stations, some of which had been overwhelmed by suburbia to become commuting stations. They would typically be double-track with a goods yard, signal-box and either a road bridge or level-crossing. Most importantly, they incorporated a two-storey station-master's house which, when combined with the station building, canopies and porches, could be melded into an integrated cluster with architectural merit. Railway architects made the most of this opportunity, creating a range of small masterpieces in timber, brick, iron and stone. A common requirement was that they should blend with their surroundings using the prevailing local materials and styles, without excessive ornamentation. The word 'vernacular' is used to describe such stations.

At the other extreme was the major terminus, mostly in London but also at Brighton. They had between four and eight approach tracks with extensive, complex pointwork and signalry serving up to twenty-two platforms. Passenger facilities were comprehensive, and included booking, waiting, left-luggage, refreshment rooms, bookstalls, mechanical departure boards, toilets, taxi ranks, bus stands, Underground access, etc. Some had adjoining hotels and Waterloo had a 'news theatre' that showed cartoons. Such stations were trainsheds, having an overall roof that enclosed the platforms, tracks and concourse – a feature also once found at certain other prestigious stations like Bournemouth, Exeter, Gosport and the two Crystal Palaces.

The vast majority of Southern stations were of small to medium size. Our pictures show a selection of such stations in the styles of Classical, Tudor-Gothic, Italianate, French Renaissance, Cottage Orné, Old English, Domestic Revival and some in the 'vernacular' that defy formal classification. Many designs were a blend of different styles. 'Italianate' was specifically a railway term, encompassing a range of common-sense designs with hipped roofs and a rich variety of brickwork embellishments. The wealthier companies, namely the LBSCR, IWR and LSWR, tended to build more substantially than the SER, LCDR and the IWCR. Some distinctive 'company styles' emerged, taking over from the earlier 'line styles'. The SER in particular made extensive use of single-storey wooden buildings with matching signal-box. These were cheap to build and yet were enduring and charming, in sympathy with the Kentish environment.

The choice of architectural style often reflected the degree of importance of a station to the town that it served. Dorking provides an interesting contrast between the cottage style of the SER station on its east-west country route, and the grandiose style of the LBSCR station that provided a fast and frequent service to London on its north-south commuting route. Both are illustrated herein.

Visually, station buildings had three sides – road, platform and interior. Whereas the platform side held the greatest interest for steam enthusiasts, the road side held additional interest for modellers and social historians on account of the vehicles, bicycles, barrows, posters and people that could be found there. Architecturally, the road side was also the more imposing – the perfect canvas from which the railway company could impress its importance and permanence upon the local population. Our collection includes some fine station frontages, often with cars, limousines and buses, which are identified where they are prominent.

To complete the collection are a few closed stations, always of interest to railway historians and to railway artists such as Laurence Roche. Some were put to new uses, others were left to rot, but all were haunted by the ghosts of railwaymen and steam trains from long ago. They are evocative, opening the mind's eye to the life that was, to what it might have been and to what it had become. They are the Colosseum, Ephesus and Pompeii to the 'complete' railway enthusiast and the industrial archaeologist.

The station photographs portray a wealth of detail – roof types, chimney design, windows, canopy supports, valances, seats, notices, advertisements, signs, lamps, nameboards, footbridges, barrows, crossings, fences, clocks, stretcher cupboards, fire buckets, weighing machines, toilets, telegraph poles, water cranes and bridges, some of which are the subject of later chapters. Note particularly the different methods of canopy support – cantilever or post, wooden or iron, with reinforcing brackets or props.

References

1.1   Barman, C., *An Introduction to Railway Architecture*, Art and Technics Ltd, 1950.
1.2   Buck, G., *A Pictorial Survey of Railway Stations*, BCA, 1992.
1.3   Edited by Binney, M., and Pearce, D., *Railway Architecture*, SAVE Britain's Heritage, Orbis, 1979.
1.4   Biddle, G., and Nock, O.S., *The Railway Heritage of Britain*, Michael Joseph Ltd, 1983.
1.5   Biddle, G., *Victorian Stations*, David & Charles, 1973.

See also details in other chapters: LCDR, pp. 76, 92; SER, pp. 33, 49, 58, 74, 79, 92, 102, 104; LBSCR, pp. 52, 59, 77, 80, 93, 95, 121; Isle of Wight, pp. 73, 98; LSWR, pp. 2, 40, 41, 77, 93, 95, 115, 124.

Ludgate Hill served the City on what is now the 'Thameslink' line. Opened by the LCDR in 1864, it was rebuilt by the SECR in 1910 as a single island platform. After closure in 1929, it remained for decades – unpainted, neglected and decaying, with rusting steelwork and broken drain-pipes. The station was photographed in 1959, its faded posters from the 1920s evoking happy memories of summer holidays and day-trips to the coastal resorts of Seaford and Deal. The lower notice-boards no doubt carried timetables, on either side of what was probably a waiting-room. One can still sense the bowler-hatted commuters during the rush-hours.

The surface railways of inner London were built mostly upon brick viaducts whose arches accommodated a wealth of small industries and businesses. Below Brixton station, a market atmosphere prevails with shops, a stall-holder's barrow and parked motorbikes. Tubular steel columns support the platforms, staircase and (right) the LBSCR's South London line. Opened by the LCDR in 1862, Brixton once had branch platforms for workmen's trains running between Victoria and Ludgate Hill. Although 'modernised' during the SR electrification programme of the mid-1920s, Brixton station retained an air of antiquity.

Country stations on the LCDR main line were cheap and basic. At Meopham, the station-master's house was detached from the wooden station building. Ordinariness was relieved only by the bargeboards and valances. Electrified in 1939, the platforms were extended in 1959 and the goods yard was closed.

The LCDR terminus at Sheerness-on-Sea was rebuilt in 1883. Although the deep valancing is pure LCDR, the single-storey, hipped-roofed, weather-boarded design was copied from the SER. The name-sign is BR. The motor cars are an Austin 16 (left), two Armstrong Siddeley limousines and a Ford Anglia. *The Star* was one of three London evening newspapers from that era.

Herne Hill was an elevated junction where LCDR trains once divided for Victoria and the City. Opened in
1862, the platforms were remodelled in 1925 as Up and Down 'islands'. The 'flying albatross' shape of the
canopy was also favoured by the SECR. The tower of the original building is in the background. Light
Pacific No. 34001 *Exeter* runs through with empty stock for Victoria.

The SECR built few new stations, but Whitstable & Tankerton was rebuilt in 1915 in Classical style using
red brick and Portland stone. It gives a neat, functional, compact appearance with an underlying message of
permanence and dependability. Similar buildings served the Up and Down sides.

Cliffe typifies the small SER country station building, featuring a single storey of Kentish clapboard upon a brick base. The roof is hipped and the platform canopy is arced. The windows are less typical, having two large panes. Note the pollarded trees, ornate oil lanterns and the stationman's pre-war car.

The Hastings line had buildings designed by William Tress. Wadhurst was Italianate, framed here by the lattice footbridge and Dutton signal-box. Note the staggered platforms, barrow crossing, long Up siding, shunting disc and Railway Executive enamelled sign. A flat-sided DMU departs for Hastings.

Engineered by Colonel Stephens, Hawkhurst had a cheap type of SER building using galvanised corrugated
steel for the wall cladding and roof. The platform canopy is integral with the gabled roof. The paling fence is
the same as at Cliffe but the windows have the more usual SER arrangement of four panes.

The Up platform canopy at Dorking Town had an SER arc roof with iron posts. It was reached by subway.
Built on a gentle curve, a banner repeater was provided for the starting signal. The staggered platforms gave a
neat arrangement of sidings but their overlap made the staff crossing unsuitable for barrows.

The SER's use of corrugated steel was repeated at Canterbury South on the Elham Valley line to Folkestone. Opened in 1887–9 to keep the LCDR at bay, the line was closed in 1947. Seen here in 1959, the station building has become a private residence with a filled-in garden between the platforms.

Certain stations on the SER's Guildford line were in the Cottage Orné style. This is Dorking Town, with steeply pitched roofs, ornate gables but with a plain brick lower half and an undecorated canopy. The telegraph lines take a short-cut across the front of the building. The goods shed has been enlarged and the goods siding is unusual, being integrated with the station forecourt.

Between Peckham Rye and London Bridge, the LBSCR's South London line had three tracks, the centre track used for empty stock working. It was an elevated railway, whose stations were exposed and draughty. South Bermondsey was rebuilt in 1928 with an island platform in place of the old centre track. The steel bridge (left) spanned the approach tracks to Bricklayers Arms goods station.

Dorking North was a large LBSCR station in the Italianate style. A sense of balance was created by the linked pavilions with single-storey wings. Note the different styles of window, the elaborate porch valancing and some odd chimney extensions. In waiting are two Humber Super Snipes and three hikers.

When the Crystal Palace was relocated in 1854, the LBSCR served it with a new branch from Sydenham. This was soon extended to Wandsworth, Norwood Junction and Beckenham Junction and became a hub of the great suburban complex. From the 1860s to the turn of the century, the LBSCR rebuilt many of its larger stations in a lavish, substantial French or Italian style with a clerestoried booking hall. Rising majestically in the leafy suburbs, the Crystal Palace (low-level) of 1875 also had a fine carriage canopy (*porte cochère*) with ornate ironwork. Triumphal stone staircases led to the platforms below. Overall, the station was as sublime as a Mahler symphony.

During the 1880s the LBSCR built a batch of substantial country stations in the High Weald of Sussex in Norman Shaw's Old English style. This is Rotherfield & Mark Cross, whose wide platform canopy is echoed by a smaller one on the Up side. Note the motor bike by the S&F wooden signal-box. It was always a pleasure to use such beautiful stations.

Hailsham was the principal town on the 'Cuckoo' line and was originally a terminus for the short branch from Polegate. The single-storey buildings are unusual for the LBSCR. They have a restful, symmetrical arrangement of linked pavilions, their common roof-line broken only by the Tudor chimney stacks.

East Grinstead had a large building in Old English style – tall chimneys, mullioned windows and red-brick walls, partly hung with courses of plain and fish-scale tiles. Sited on the Down side of the low-level, this was the start of the Bluebell line. The 'lowbridge' M&D bus to Tonbridge is an AEC Regent V. Sadly, BR demolished these lovely buildings, replaced by a mundane single-storey hut.

Grange Road was one of many rural LBSCR stations that were optimistically large. This asymmetric pavilion layout was repeated at many other stations, but Grange Road was exceptional for its fine brickwork. Note especially the chimneys, projections below the roof-line, variegated courses and window arches.

The LBSCR terminus of Bognor Regis was rebuilt in 1902 in Domestic Revival style. C. Hamilton Ellis described it as 'super-suburban'. It might also be mistaken for a school. There are no half-timbered gables usually associated with Domestic Revival, but the mini-gables, dormer windows, chimney arrangements and clock tower are delightful. A sense of extravagance is enhanced by the long canopy and the huge BR enamelled sign. The Ford Prefect (left) dates from the immediate post-war years while the shiny Morris Minor is a late 1950s model. Overall, there is a sense of seaside welcome.

Old coaches were sometimes used for additional staff accommodation. This SECR coach is isolated in a bay at Chichester, displaying its end detail. Note the LBSCR valancing and the faded black-and-white bands on the posts, a relic of the war-time blackout. The bikes presumably belonged to railwaymen.

Langston's platform and fence posts have been renewed in pre-fabricated concrete. The LBSCR nameboard, however, with its metal letters, has been retained, so too the LBSCR seat. This type of wooden building with corrugated roof was also found at North Hayling and along the south coast.

Opposite: Bembridge was the terminus of the Brading Harbour branch. Its station building was long and two storied, with Tudor chimneys and some ornate gables. The platform canopy was exceptionally long and wide, almost obscuring the tiny wooden signal-box, set back from the platform with a tunnel below the platform for the rods and wires. The branch opened in 1882, primarily to serve a new quay at St Helens from which a minerals only train-ferry operated until 1888 to Langston Harbour. The branch was worked by the IWR, taken over by them in 1898 and closed in 1953.

Mill Hill was a simple rectangular 'barn' of a station on the outskirts of Cowes. The brickwork, bargeboards and wall-propped canopy were nevertheless pleasing. Platform provisions included a bunker, stretcher cupboard and three different styles of seat. Note the immaculate whitening of the lower brickwork, platform edge and tunnel portal, no doubt contending for the 'Best Kept Station' award.

Opposite: Horringford was on the IWCR's Sandown line. Its simple building was unusual, having a gabled loft window and looking more like a farm building. The tiny signal-box reminds us that it was a station and the Home signal remains diligently at 'stop'. The concrete platform appears to have been cast *in situ*. The line closed in 1956. By the time this photograph was taken four years later, the track had been dismantled, and was awaiting removal.

Sir William Tite's country stations for the Southampton line were in bold Italianate style, as seen at St Denys
– an imperial mansion in brick, stone and slate. The great wooden canopy, with neat valancing, iron posts
and brackets, protects three seats, a bike, stretcher cupboard and a passenger weighing machine. More
modern features are the pre-cast concrete platform edge, the BR enamelled signs and the flat-bottom track.
Except for one lady with a suitcase, passengers' eyes are upon the 'Union Castle Express', charging through
behind an unidentified 'Schools' class 4–4–0.

The Tudor dignity of Axminster by Sir William Tite. A sense of height is provided by the steep-pitched roofs, great gables and extended chimneys. The cluster of offices and mullioned windows bring a sense of depth and dependability. The porch behind the taxi leads to the station-master's house.

Axminster's Tudor dignity extended to the single-storey wooden rooms on the Up side, with their twin gables, ornate bargeboards and finials. There was no canopy, presumably because of the water column. The platforms were semi-staggered and the angled road bridge was a masterpiece of masonry.

Chandlers Ford was built as a cluster of small rooms and out-buildings, weather-boarded and slate-roofed.
The brick 'gents' and concrete fence came later. Drain vents compete with the forest of chimneys. The
peaceful scene is enhanced by a cat resting beneath the LSWR luggage barrow.

The railway side of Chandlers Ford had a waiting area with a
heavy LSWR canopy, cantilevered to the edge of the platform.
The end window gave protection to a weighing machine,
bicycle, some scattered parcels and the imaginary passengers.
Further along are an LSWR seat and a four-wheeled barrow.

Opened in 1854, the LWSR's North Devon line had stone-built stations in Tudor style to the design of Sir William Tite. This is King's Nympton, seen in full summer colours with wisteria along the porch. The main building and station-master's house are at the same end, an unusual arrangement. Note the posters, simple bench, LSWR barrow, oil lantern, enamelled SR signs and the platform bell. It was a delight to pause here on the Torrington section of the 'Atlantic Coast Express'.

Oakley was a stopping station on the West of England main line. It had short platforms, a large building and no footbridge. There was a coal siding at the country end and a goods platform and siding at the London end (right). Traffic receipts were modest but the rural setting was sublime.

Daggons Road was a semi-forgotten two-storey station on the single-track line from Salisbury to Bournemouth. It had rose bushes, LSWR oil lanterns and wooden cut-out letters for the nameboard and other signs. Points for two sidings were operated from a ground-frame in the tiny signal-box (right).

Yarde was a one-coach halt on the Torrington–Halwill line. Opened by the SR in 1925, prefabricated concrete was used for the platform, name-sign, shelter and fence posts. Lanterns are missing from the cast-iron lamp standards. The rural setting, with grocer's van and rolling hills, is a delight.

Chilsworthy was on the PD&SWJR Callington branch which opened in 1909. The platform and bridge abutments are of local Dartmoor stone but the shelter is wooden. Two oil-lamps were operated by a guard. Such a halt would enhance any model railway, perhaps leading to a fiddle yard on the right.

A detail from Herne Bay, where ornate iron brackets support the wooden beams of the platform canopy. Cast as separate components, the four brackets are bolted to each other and to the beams above. The hexagonal iron post has an ornate top that obscures the transition to the brackets.

Some fine detail on the front wall of West Hoathly station. The flush-mounted letter-box is cast with VR . The stonework incorporates the gutter, the LBSCR monogram, the date of opening and three floral motifs. The top window on the right is stained in twin circular patterns.

YARDS, SHEDS AND HUTS

During the Victorian era, railways had near monopolies of both passenger and freight traffic. There was some lingering competition from the inland waterways and coasters, but the major competition for freight was between different railway companies serving the same towns. The SR experienced increasing competition from lorries but it was not until after Nationalisation that long-distance road transport became dominant. The building of the motorway network accelerated the decline of rail freight, culminating in the end of the pick-up goods train and the closure of local goods yards. The final years of BR steam therefore coincided with the demise of local freight, leading to extinction. Goods trains and yards were a colourful part of the steam railway scene, adding variety and texture, especially in the electrified areas. Half-hidden corners of yards held many surprises for the intrepid photographer-enthusiast, including several old coaches featured in Chapter Seven.

During the early 1960s most passenger stations still had associated yards for the loading, unloading, storing, weighing and recording of general goods and coal. Regular pick-up goods trains would call at the yards, while long-distance goods trains would be assembled and disassembled at the junctions and strategically placed marshalling yards. Inter-company transfers were a major part of the freight business – the railways worked as one organisation in that respect, evidence of which lies in the labels and documentation recorded in Chapter Eight. The Maunsell utility van provided further evidence of this – an ambassador of the Southern whose distinctive shape and panelling could be 'spotted' in most parts of Great Britain.

In the London area, there were major marshalling yards at Feltham (LSWR), Norwood (LBSCR) and Hither Green (SECR) for inter-railway transfers. The major London goods stations were at Nine Elms (LSWR), Blackfriars (LCDR), Bricklayers Arms (SER/ LBSCR) and Battersea (LBSCR). Each had a huge fleet of lorries (originally horse-drawn carts) for delivery and collection of parcels in the Central London area, while some customers used their own road transport. Both Nine Elms and Bricklayers Arms incorporated former passenger stations. Two sheds at Nine Elms are featured in this chapter, each with an assortment of lorries. One was the train shed of the LSWR's original London passenger terminus. It had a classical frontage designed by Sir William Tite, similar to Southampton Terminus at the other end of the line. Gosport and Ashford West are further examples of passenger stations that became goods only.

Our pictures show the local goods yard both as a whole and in detail. We find loading gauges, coal stores, loading docks and substantial goods sheds of timber, brick and stone, built for weather-protected loading and storage. Private sheds and old wagon bodies were also used for storage. Some yards were tucked behind the station, incorporating the platform bay, while others were located beyond the platforms, making a long layout overall. A sad feature of many of the pictures is the air of neglect, and the grass growing in the now deserted yards. We were witnessing the end of an era, the demise of an institution.

Some small goods yards were used for overnight storage of passenger coaches but the larger stations had special yards for the storage and servicing of coaches. Finding enough storage in London for commuter trains was a particular problem, and the scheduling of empty stock workings was a work of art. Electric multiple unit (EMU) storage and cleaning sidings are featured in pictures taken at Crystal Palace, Fratton and Portsmouth.

Storage yards were used for lineside industries, railway works and Motive Power Depots (MPDs). There was fruit from Hawkhurst, milk from Torrington, fish from Padstow and military equipment from Wool. Yards were also used for storage of service trains such as weed-killing and mobile cranage, not to mention railway equipment and piles of old wooden sleepers – a jumble of railway memorabilia between huts, weighbridges and roadways.

Major MPDs like Exmouth Junction had huge coaling towers – energy stores for trains running to London and the far west – plus sidings for both locomotives and coal. Branch termini, on the other hand, had just one or two sidings for locomotive storage and servicing, with a modest coal store served periodically by a single wagon. Sometimes the locomotive siding was integral with the goods yard, as at Lyme Regis, but segregation was a neater arrangement. The layout at Margate Sands MPD is obscure, it having closed in 1926.

Finally there are the huts used for lamp oil, platelayers' trolleys and the platelayers themselves – that is to say, for messing and for storage of their equipment. Huts were constructed from a variety of materials, ranging from timber planks and old tar-infused sleepers to concrete and corrugated steel. The wooden ones were cheap but a fire hazard on account of sparks from steam locomotives; the others were more expensive but fire-proof. Examples are shown of each type, but the SR is probably best remembered for its ubiquitous prefabricated concrete hut.

See also details in other chapters: goods sheds, pp. 9, 11, 13, 114; loading docks, pp. 26, 65; engine sheds, pp. 99, 123; water towers, pp. 61, 63; loading gauge, p. 78; EMU sidings, pp. 95, 119, 120; water cranes, pp. viii, 23, 66, 88, 89, 99, 116; huts, pp. 48, 49, 52, 73, 77, 78.

A push-pull train approaches Hawkhurst terminus, headed by SECR 0–4–4 tank No. 31266. Agricultural traffic was the life-blood of the line, including seasonal hop-pickers' specials from London Bridge. The branch opened in 1893 and closed in 1961. Here in the summer of 1959, the SER two-road engine shed is disused and the goods yard is largely redundant and overgrown with grass – note the heaps of rotting sleepers. The steel signal bracket, lattice dolls, corrugated arms and cast-iron 'Warning' sign are SR.

Ashford West terminus was opened by the LCDR in 1884 but relegated to goods only status following the SECR merger of 1899. Sixty years on, the old platforms, now grassy, have plenty of space for loading from lorries and drays. There is a large goods shed on the right with the original goods yard on the left. Such major investments ensured that the LCDR remained crippled financially.

Margate Sands was a remote outpost of the SER, reached via Ashford and reversal at Ramsgate. It closed in 1926 as part of the Thanet rationalisation. The station building became an amusement arcade while the engine shed, seen here in 1959, became a warehouse. Locomotives are left to the imagination.

Formerly Clapham Bus Garage, the Museum of British Transport opened in 1961. Just arriving is
Metropolitan 2–4–0 tank No. 23, restored in maroon livery. Centre-stage is 4–4–0 class D No. 737 in SECR
green with brass dome, built in 1901 for express passenger duties. Exhibits have since transferred to the
NRM, York, and to the LT Museum, Covent Garden.

As safety precautions, the lamp room at Hawkhurst was made of corrugated steel and vented. Alongside is a
platelayers' trolley hut of timber construction. Note the chain connecting the SECR ground-signal to the
run-round point. The platform lamp is SER and stored utility vans are SR Maunsell.

SER loading gauges had three central suspended rods, as seen at Cliffe. Note the tarpaulins and semaphore ground-signal, a yellow arm with black bar, for exiting the siding onto the running line. The signalling is SR, probably renewed around 1932 when the line was extended to Allhallows-on-Sea.

The local coal supply service at Brasted: a standard 16 ton steel open wagon; a heap of 'smalls'; a mobile coal-weigher for tipping into sacks; and an old wooden covered van, bereft of wheels but elevated on timber and brick piles, used for dry storage and loading of sacks onto the coal lorry.

Goods sheds were often located in the bay of country stations. This one at Baynards provides the perfect
shelter and sun-trap for the growing of dahlias. Note the wooden crane within the shed, the oil lantern on
the wall and the LBSCR signal post with SR arm. A lone goods van stands in the yard.

For run-through facilities with a loop, goods sheds were best located in yards beyond the station. Sadly, this
weather-boarded shed at Cowden is closed, with corrugated sheets across the door. Note the SR concrete
loading gauge, sleeper-built platelayers' hut and rich woodland around Markbeech tunnel.

General features of LSWR platelayers' huts were the vertical wood panelling and beading and a steeply pitched gabled roof. This small example was photographed near Lyme Regis, its functional dignity enhanced by a briar rose, rustic fence, a roll of fencing wire, metal cans and a new chimney. All that it lacks is a window!

This large LSWR platelayers' hut near Oakley looks more like a scene from the American Wild West. Exceptionally tall with a brick stack and a lean-to shelter, only the horses are missing at the 'OK Corral'. Such huts were used for both shelter and storage. What tales were told around the fire in mid-winter?

Pre-Group platelayers' huts were generally wooden with a brick chimney. Their frequent fate was to burn down, a problem resolved by the SR prefabricated concrete version. They blended well with the countryside! This one is on the Medway Valley line, seen with a local train from Maidstone West.

Nine Elms was the LSWR's London terminus until 1848 when it became goods only. The original timber roof-trusses and cast-iron columns were still evident in 1961. For parcels traffic, the Scammell Scarab 'mechanical horse' was a familiar sight on major railways – this is the post-war 'rounded' version.

Wool had goods sidings to either side of the main line. The army lorries (right) are from Bovington camp. 'Merchant Navy' class Pacific No. 35008 *Orient Line* restarts from the station with an Up train from Weymouth.

This purpose-built goods shed at Nine Elms had a multiplicity of iron roof-trusses and rows of jib cranes.
The cobbled road was designed for horse-drawn vehicles, much shorter than Bill Nash's Bedford 'artic',
which almost occupies the full width. Note the tall desk and the 'mechanical horse' open trailer.

Many LSWR main line goods yards were entered via a double-slip point, as seen here at Shawford. The yard
is overgrown and looks disused. A light Pacific passes with a Down Bournemouth express. The relief road
beyond the telegraph poles comes off the Winchester Chesil line.

Gosport was the terminus of the LSWR's first extension, opening in 1840. Its two platforms were for goods
(left) and passengers (right). It became goods only in 1953 and closed in 1969. Maunsell 0–6–0–class Q
No. 30536 shunts below the post-war roof. The original overall roof was destroyed by incendiary bomb in 1941.

This carriage-washing shed is at Fratton. A 4-car 'Pompey' EMU stands in a former goods siding with
loading bays. There was once an island platform here, the start of the East Southsea branch which closed in
1914. Beyond the level-crossing, EMUs are stored where Drummond motor trains once plied.

A busy scene at Torrington with Ivatt 2–6–2 tanks heading two Barnstaple trains of Bulleid stock. A milk dock is by the goods shed, with fillers for three tanks and pumps in the reception shed alongside. The goods shed and station are built of local stone, but the dark engine shed beyond is wooden.

The railway at Wadebridge ran through the centre of town, between a jumble of huts and buildings. Looking towards Padstow, the original Bodmin & Wadebridge engine shed and workshop are on the left. The weighbridge has interlaced tracks to avoid over-use of the mechanisms. The wooden hut (right) is LSWR.

This SR 'cenotaph' coaling tower at Exmouth Junction MPD was visible for miles around. Here was the stored energy for all the Waterloo expresses and trains to the Atlantic coast. The great ferro-concrete bunker with its steel hood had balance weights to either side of the hoist. In the siding are wooden and steel open wagons of up to 16 tons capacity, one of which is being hoisted for tipping. Note the exceptionally tall water tower beyond the 'serrated' roof of the great engine shed.

In contrast to the Exmouth Junction 'cenotaph' is the simple wooden coaling staithe at Hayling Island, located on the engine run-round loop. Coaling here was manual, with the larger lumps stacked at the sides to retain the 'smalls' in the centre. Note the substantial goods shed beyond the SR brake van. The charm of this branch lay in the contrasts of scales. The long line of coal wagons, for example, looks far too heavy for the diminutive 'Terrier' tanks.

The original goods yard at Callington had some odd corners between pre-railway buildings. This double siding arrangement looks surreal – the neat trackwork, tidy coal heaps and massive corrugated roof contrasting with the ancient rough-stone warehouses with their sagging roofs.

Padstow was the western-most terminus of the LSWR. Its locomotive facilities were basic, comprising a water tower, water crane, ash-pit and a turntable jutting into the sea – enlarged in 1947 to accommodate the Bulleid Pacifics. Locomotives would run light to Wadebridge for coaling, overnight stabling and light maintenance. Padstow's South Quay was completed in 1910 for increased fish traffic; it is being used here for overnight storage of a Bulleid set, propelled by Drummond 4–4–0 class T9 No. 30338. Note the grounded coach bodies, one of which is featured on page 115.

Chapter Three

SIGNALS AND SIGNAL-BOXES

In the days of BR steam, three families of signal could be found on the Southern: pre-Group semaphore (two-position, mostly lower-quadrant); SR semaphore (two-position, upper-quadrant); and SR/ BR colour-lights (three- or four-aspect). Pre-Group signal arms were generally wooden, but many of these had been replaced by SR pressed-steel arms, creating hybrids.

Victorian signal posts were mostly wooden and therefore had a tendency to rot, but some survived into the 1960s. The LCDR and LSWR adopted the more durable lattice steel posts, whose designs were perpetuated by the SECR and SR. A scattering of concrete posts could also be found, together with hundreds of cheap rail-built posts from the 1930s. Colour-lights were generally mounted on tubular steel posts. All companies used distinctive iron finials for their mechanical signal posts, the SR adopting the LSWR spiked pattern except on rail-built posts, which had the flat rectangular SR cap. All types are illustrated herein.

A 'signal bracket' is defined as having one or more 'dolls' (top-posts) set upon a gallery with a single support post (or cluster of posts). The purpose of the bracket is to support a multiplicity of signals and/or to offset the signal to one side for improved visibility. Brackets could be left- or right-handed or 'balanced'. With posts made of wood, the SECR and LBSCR used distinctive iron angles to support the gallery. With steel posts, on the other hand, reinforcement at the angles was in steel, sometimes of intricate lattice design.

Signal structures are called 'gantries' when they span the tracks with support at either side. They were generally of lattice or braced steel design, sometimes gracefully arched and sometimes cantilevered over the furthermost track(s). Many gantries could be found on the LSWR main line to Basingstoke, and they were commonly used for colour-lights, especially across four or more tracks. At junctions, brackets and gantries could support an impressive array of semaphore signals, which railway photographers strove to include in their compositions.

SR stop signal arms (home, starting, etc.) were in red with a white vertical stripe and a square end. Some pre-Group stop signals had a slight taper. Distant semaphore signals were yellow with a black chevron and a fishtail end. Lamps were oil or electric with coloured glasses – red for 'stop', green for 'clear' and amber for 'caution'. Early SR signal arms were corrugated for increased strength, but these were superseded by flat arms with ribbed edges. Short arms were common for sidings and shunting, sometimes in the same pattern as 'stop' signals but more usually in white with two red horizontal stripes. Variations of the latter were: with a red 'C' (calling-on); with a red 'S' (shunt-ahead); and plain (warning). The 'warning' could be for various hazards such as 'severe gradient ahead' or 'short section ahead'. It made the driver stop and think.

A common type of Victorian ground-signal was the revolving oil-lamp, which had a different colour for each side. Some LBSCR signals of this type survived into the mid-1960s, particularly in the rural Sussex area. The SECR introduced a miniature semaphore ground-signal, a precursor of the SR's ubiquitous Westinghouse disc type. The SR also used a Westinghouse ground-signal of the miniature semaphore type, yellow with a vertical black stripe, for exiting sidings onto a running line; this could be passed when 'on' for shunting within the sidings. Pre-Group companies also used elevated semaphore signals for entry into and exit from sidings; their short arms were red or yellow, with a black ring around a white circle.

Other bits and pieces that could be found on signal posts included route indicators (mechanical or electrical) and the distinctive white diamond which signified that the line was protected by track circuitry (showing as lights in the signal-box) so that the crew did not need to telephone the signalman when a train was held.

The Southern's predecessors were signalling pioneers. Achievements included the first fixed signals, the first train headcodes, the first signal-box, the first semaphores, the first distant signals, the fishtail end, interlocking of points with signals, full interlocking, block working, the lock-and-block system, semaphore block instruments, track circuitry, power signalling, automatic train signalling and the first four-aspect colour-lights (SR). John Saxby and John Farmer were originally LBSCR employees who set up their own signalling company with patents and distinctive signal-box designs (S&F). William Sykes of the LCDR invented the electric lock-and-block system, a forerunner of track circuitry.

Pre-Group railways had distinctive signal-box designs, sometimes unique to the railway and sometimes unique to the contractor. Designs evolved with time, from the elaborate Victorian timber baroque to the sleek brick and concrete designs of the SECR, SR and BR(S). The Signalling Study Group has taken infinite trouble to catalogue British signal-box types using numerals and letters (ref. 3.1). We are concerned here with those found on BR(S) during the latter days of steam. They are the author's selection, contrasting the old with the new, the tall with the dumpy, the grand with the humble.

References

3.1   The Signalling Study Group, *The Signal Box, a Pictorial History and Guide to Designs*, OPC, 1986.

3.2   Allen, D. and Woolstenholmes, C. J., *A Pictorial Survey of Railway Signalling*, OPC, 1991.

3.3   Pryer, G., *A Pictorial Record of Southern Signals*, OPC, 1977.

3.4   Vanns, M.A., *An Illustrated History of Signalling*, Ian Allan, 1997.

See also details in other chapters: LCDR post, p. 75; LBSCR posts/ arm, pp. 35, 125; LSWR/ SR lattice posts, pp. 26, 97; LSWR/ SR brackets, pp. viii, 31, 35, 73, 87, 118; LSWR/ SR gantries, pp. 86, 88; SR rail-built posts, pp. 16, 23, 34, 41, 72, 92, 94; SR route indicator, p. 92; repeaters, pp. 10, 12, 75; SECR ground-signal, p. 33; SR ground discs, pp. 11, 12, 24, 85, 92, 99, 123; SR ground semaphores, pp. 34, 116; SR arms, pp. viii, 16, 26, 31, 34, 72, 73, 75, 86, 92, 94, 97; SER boxes, pp. 11, 13, 72, 116; LBSCR boxes, pp. viii, 16, 96, 99, 117; Isle of Wight boxes, pp. 20, 73; LSWR boxes, pp. 26, 38, 77, 97, 124; BR box, p. 95; level-crossings, pp. 20, 96; telegraph poles, pp. ii, 13, 20, 26, 27, 38, 39, 97, 105, 118, 124; cable channel, p. 104.

The SECR adopted the LCDR lattice post but with a new slender 'arrow-head' finial. These stately brackets with co-acting arms guarded Bickley Junction from the west, semi-obscured by a road bridge. They date from the 1914 rationalisation of the interchange between the LCDR and SER main lines. The 4-SUB train is signalled to take the spur to Petts Wood and Orpington. Built in 1925, unit 4304 is vee-fronted, a design feature inherited from the LSWR. Civil work is in progress (right) for rebuilding the junction and for quadrupling the line to Swanley, part of the 1959 Kent Coast electrification programme.

The LCDR used lattice signal-posts together with a broad-leaf spiked finial. This example at Herne Hill Sorting Sidings holds an SR siding signal. Note the assorted sheds, raised walkways, bucket, benches, etc., which tend to accumulate in goods yards. An SR utility van from the Maunsell era stands on the right.

SECR shunting signals were miniature semaphores – lower quadrant with a red arm and white stripe. They were chain-operated from the front end with a generous overhang for the balance weight. The oil-lamp looks taller than the signal itself on this perfectly preserved example at Hawkhurst.

Cranbrook station had a delightful setting on a natural curve in the High Weald, seen here with a push-pull train. The facing point of the run-round loop was protected by an elevated SR shunting disc and by a lockbar on the track (depressed by wheel flanges to prevent point operation). The Up home signal arm is SR steel, beginning to rust, bolted to the stub of an older arm. The iron finial, wooden doll and bracket are SECR. They are located on the 'wrong' side of the track for improved visibility on the curve. Three wooden huts beyond are respectively for platelayers, their trolley and coal.

Opposite: The LBSCR's suburban system was complex. Here at Sutton, a post-war 4-SUB unit from Epsom is departing for Mitcham Junction, beneath an SR lattice 'gallows' bracket with suspended signals. The foreground signals are also SR but mounted on a steel cantilevered gantry of LBSCR design with its distinctive finial caps and wooden dolls. The cast-iron 'ring' of the angle was used by the LBSCR, SER and other railways. Note the 20 mph speed restriction for trains coming off the Epsom Downs branch, also the SR 'barley sugar' electric lamp standard with EMU stop-signs. See page 83 for the locomotive *Sutton*.

LBSCR signal posts were wooden, tapered, of square-section with a squat, unsharp finial cap. Arms were wooden, lower quadrant and oil-lit, although this one has apparently been electrified. This post near Grange Road is painted white except for black preservative near the base. The distant arm is faded. Note the mechanism of crank, chain, balance arm and turnbuckle adjuster.

The branch terminus of Hayling Island, featuring a 'Terrier' tank and two Maunsell coaches. Photographed in 1961, the starting signals are a mix of BR(S) rail-built and LBSCR wooden. The signal-box is small and simple, with a separate refuge hut for the signalman (right), partly obscured by roses.

Many nineteenth-century ground-signals were revolving oil-lamps. This LBSCR survivor at Rowfant was waist-high. When 'set', the engine crew saw the green face with the white cross. Note the timber platelayers' hut, probably of LBSCR vintage.

Hayling Island signal-box with its ground-frame, telegraph, clock, fire buckets, bicycle and wallflower. The wooden LBSCR lower-quadrant starting signal is slightly tapered, soon to be replaced (see opposite).

The wooden signal-box for the 'B' ground-frame at Callington. The SR steel starting signal is lower quadrant on a PD&SWJR square wooden post with a pointed finial of 'open diamond' design. This signal assembly would soon suffer the same fate as that at Hayling Island – to be replaced by one of SR rail-built design. Exactly fifty years old, its life had no doubt been prolonged by the reinforcement post at the base.

The LSWR was a pioneer of power-operated signals. This gantry at Basingstoke, with pneumatic starting signals, served from 1912 until 1966. The Up train is headed by rebuilt 'Merchant Navy' class Pacific No. 35005 *Canadian Pacific*, contrasting with the nose of an air-smoothed 'Battle of Britain'. Two foreground posts have both lost their signs, no doubt warning not to trespass.

A cantilevered gantry dating from the 1935 remodelling of Tonbridge. The dolls and finials are a mix of SR types. The central group comprises: starter for the Sevenoaks line; shunting disc; entry to sidings; and a raised starter for Redhill. Light Pacific No. 34037 *Clovelly* heads a train of BR Mark 1 coaches.

This pair of fixed-distant signals was installed mid-way between Havant and Langston. The SR practice of using old bullhead rails as signal posts was perpetuated by BR(S).

A concrete signal post near Deepdene, believed to be of SR vintage but based on an LBSCR design. Such posts were not entirely successful, as fixings were constrained to the pre-cast holes. A train of Maunsell stock passes by.

A heavily laden SR left-hand bracket at Tulse Hill. The centre doll for Streatham has 'distant' colour-lights and a ringed signal for entry into sidings. The left doll for West Norwood and the right doll for Streatham Hill each have a Warning signal with a side indicator to show 'W' when 'off'. Trains had to stop here before proceeding with caution to 'on' stop signals that guarded the junctions on the short spurs ahead. Note the SR 'roundel' totem name-sign, mounted on the gas lamp standard.

This SR 'balanced' bracket dates from 1932 and the opening of the branch terminus of Allhallows-on-Sea. The gallery is supported on old rails with lattice cantilevers, holding four lattice dolls with spiked finials. The central pair of 'splitting' home signals are for the island platform. Their long flat arms contrast with the shorter, corrugated arms for entry to the sidings on either side. This flat landscape, with a few brick buildings and a scattering of caravans, fully reflects the bleakness of the Hoo peninsular. The Allhallows sub-branch was popular for day trips from London (see page 142) but it did not survive the Beeching inquisition.

Groombridge was blessed with island Down platforms, reached by subway. Because of platform curvature, this SR bracket was greatly cantilevered, with steadying guys from the post on the right. The canopy awning is of late LBSCR 'loping' design and the BR signal-box beyond is brick with a flat roof.

High Halstow halt had an SER wooden signal-box with a brick closet behind. It served the level-crossing and a private siding. The gates are standard SR, having 'X' bracing and hung upon concrete posts.

Most SER signal-boxes were in company style (the same as SER single-storey buildings) using Kentish clapboard, a hipped roof and windows of Georgian proportions (see page 11). Unlike other railways, they had vertical sash-cord windows. This is Ashford C, complete with brick base, fire buckets and coal store. The visitors are students in railway history from Goldsmiths College, London. Their leader has a rolled umbrella and bowler hat, symbols of middle management when on the line. Note the tall concrete yard lamp with 'art deco' bracket.

Elmers End signal-box was smaller than Ashford C, but with a WC on stilts. It pre-dates and faces away from the Hayes branch, seen here with a train of EPB stock. The Mid Kent line opened from Lewisham to Beckenham Junction in 1857. It was extended to Addiscombe Road in 1864 and to Hayes in 1882.

The signal-box at Hawkhurst was of McKenzie & Holland design, opened in 1893. Its finials, gabled roof and small window panes contrast with SER in-house designs. The water tower alongside has aesthetic merit by virtue of its multi-coloured bricks, cornices and round-topped windows and door.

Both the LCDR and LBSCR used Saxby &
Farmer signal-boxes predominantly. Chatham is a
large example, seen here in grimy condition after
closure in 1959. It is weather-boarded with a
hipped roof and rectangular windows – two panes
deep with rounded corners and a row of narrow
top-lights.

Canterbury East signal-box was similar to Chatham
except that it was elevated on stilts and still clean,
nicely painted in cream and green. There was a WC at
the top of the long staircase. The old starter signal
bracket has an LCDR finial. Its replacement bracket
beyond has finials of LSWR/ SR pattern.

Another type of S&F signal-box had a gabled roof with a pronounced overhang at the front and back. Examples could be found on both the SER and LCDR. This is Ravensbourne, built upon a brick base and with an ornate ridge. Despite the cat-walk, the windows are filthy, for the box is closed.

This tall signal-box at Herne Hill Sorting Sidings was of LCDR in-house design, having vertical boarding, small finials, and windows three panes deep. It looks in need of maintenance – with bent railings and faded, peeling paint – but the windows are gleaming, evidence of continuing use.

Four-aspect colour-light signals were found mainly on electrified lines. In 1960 Denmark Hill had BR colour-lights on the Catford Loop (LCDR) but SR semaphores on the South London line (LBSCR). The hipped roof, 'spiked' finial-ventilator, large overhang and awnings make the S&F signal-box enchanting.

Two general features of early LSWR signal-boxes were the hipped roof and small window panes. This variation on Camelford's platform had a multiplicity of panes, five deep. It was brick-built upon a stone plinth, with a short brick staircase. It dated from the opening of the North Cornwall line in 1893.

This Saxby & Farmer signal-box at Bexhill Central was brick-built. Its hipped roof and window arrangement were similar to many on the LCDR. Approaching from the west is a train of 2-HAL units, introduced in 1939. There are sidings to either side, including a fenced end-loading dock.

Late LSWR signal-boxes (from about 1895) were quite different from their predecessors, having a central brick (or stone) pillar and tall window panes, two deep, curved at the top. This is Gosport, sadly closed with its nameboard missing and the locking room apertures blocked. Note the token-exchange platform.

Bickley Junction signal-box dates from the SECR rationalisation of 1914. It looks more modern than LCDR/ S&F types, having full brickwork and a narrow band of windows. The men are working on the 1959 improvements of the line to Swanley. The gantry is for impending colour-light signals.

Early SR signal-boxes incorporated features of the principal pre-Group companies. From 1929, design was standardised with a gabled roof and a high glazing bar. Dover Priory box dates from 1930, part of the station re-modelling. The WC is to the right. Steaming past is Bulleid 0–6–0 class Q1 No. 33037.

In 1935 the SR introduced its 'modern' style of brick and concrete signal-box, also called 'glasshouse', 'Odeon' or 'streamlined'. It had a rounded upper storey, a flat roof with a large overhang, large window panes, a long lower storey and a vivid name panel in relief. Portsmouth Harbour box was built in 1946.

Exmouth Junction had a pre-1880 LSWR signal-box - tall with a narrow band of small windows, just two panes deep. The long wooden staircase led to a porch with closet. Weather-boarded upon a stone plinth, it was twice extended in brick to house forty-nine levers. It was replaced in 1959 by a new mechanical box of sixty-four levers, engineered by BR(S) in modern materials with a flat roof and a brick base.

SIGNS, LAMPS AND SEATS

Cast-iron signs were enduring, being resistant to rust and knocks. They needed regular painting, however, for legibility and corrosion protection. Such signs were still common in the 1950s and '60s, particularly from the SER, SECR, EKR, LSWR and SR. They looked splendid in Southern green or red, with the letters and edges picked out in white, a time-consuming task. While some were simple warning notices of danger or trespass, others were detailed legal or procedural notices, concerning rights of way, trespass, damage and crossings.

Steel enamelled signs were less enduring than cast iron, being prone to chips and scratches, particularly around the screw holes, leading to terminal corrosion. The LBSCR used enamelled signs and few have survived. They were cheap to produce, however, and the SR used them also, perpetuated by BR(S). The Southern's 'Don't touch conductor rails' in red letters on a white ground was a classic. Also common in the electrified areas were the enamelled stop-signs for 4, 6, 8 cars, etc. (S = all train lengths).

For posts, steel was preferable to wood as it ensured a long life. Old rail was especially durable. Telegraph poles were the exception, being almost always timber. The SR introduced steel-reinforced concrete posts for all types of sign, including cast station name-signs. If knocked, however, such posts could fracture, causing corrosion of the internal steel. Crumpled, flaking, decaying concrete posts are a sad sight. But pre-cast concrete was cheap and was used for platform components, footbridges, huts, ballast bins, gradient signs, mileposts and bridge numbers. They came from the LSWR's concrete works at Exmouth Junction, which was extended and greatly exploited by the SR.

Pre-Group station name-signs were generally either painted or in metal or wooden cut-out letters upon a wooden board, a number of which survived into BR days. They were largely replaced by SR enamelled signs, in some cases mounted on an original pre-Group wooden board. Small enamelled station name-signs (totems) of the SR 'roundel' type became commonplace, particularly on lamp standards. These were superseded by the BR enamelled totem of 'double sausage' style. At larger stations and junctions, train destination boards might be found, to be slotted into a platform post by the porter.

Platform lamps and standards were essentially the same as those found in city streets and on prominent buildings. Victorian station lamps were fuelled mostly by oil, and at rural stations and halts oil remained king into the 1960s. Maintenance of the lamps required a ladder for the daily chores of filling, wick-trimming and glass cleaning. Of the four large faces, the front one was hinged and often bore the name of the station. Oil lanterns were tapered, the SER and LCDR versions having a particularly narrow waist. Mounting variations included suspension, side-bracket or directly onto a standard.

Although some early city stations were lit by gas flame, gas was not in widespread use until after 1886 when the incandescent mantle first appeared. Gas was easier to operate and maintain than oil, having a permanent pilot flame and requiring only a pole to operate the main burner. Gas lamps were mostly suspended at the top through their tap, using a cradle, swan-neck or arm. Early gas lamps were converted oil lanterns, then came the Sugg Rochester type with a glass globe beneath a wide metal brim, resembling an inverted Girl Guide hat. In the 1930s the SR introduced the hexagonal 'art deco' glass cover, which was used for both gas and electric.

The earliest electric lamps were crude, with the bulb protruding below an inverted metal saucer. Both the SR and pre-Group companies used this type; correspondence reproduced in Chapter Eight shows that electric lighting was used at London termini as early as 1905.

Regarding lamp standards, those made of wood had mostly rotted by the 1960s while those of cast iron were being gradually replaced (for reasons of fashion) by the bland BR steel tubular types. The ornamentation of standards varied between railway companies. One could find straight fluting on the LCDR and LBSCR and spiral fluting – commonly known as 'barley sugar' – on the SER and LSWR. Pre-Group companies also used a tall unfluted standard in yards (and sometimes on platforms), having a 'cradle' (divided top) to support the lamp. The SR perpetuated both the LSWR spiral design and the tall yard lamp. Then, in the 1930s, the concrete lamp standard was introduced, with modernistic 'art-deco' brackets for the lamps.

Platform lamps could be both beautiful and evocative, taking one back to ancient ways of life. The hiss and flicker of gas lamps was particularly eerie on deserted platforms. The standards too were interesting, often supporting a variety of accessories including name-signs, loudspeakers, wires, cables and telegraph spars.

Platform seats were similar to those found in municipal parks and gardens. Details varied from company to company but they generally had a slatted back with a slatted or bench seat, held together on three iron frames, sometimes mounted on wooden skids. Some were embellished with cast-iron railway monograms. Simple wooden benches or 'pews' could also be found, especially in shelters and waiting-rooms.

The illustrations show various other platform accoutrements including weighing machines, stretcher cupboards, fire buckets, clocks, signal bells and barrows. Hand barrows may be classified into four main types: two small wheels for light luggage; two large wheels with leaf springs for heavier baggage; four small wheels with two ends, commonly used for mail; and four large wheels with leaf springs for parcels and mail.

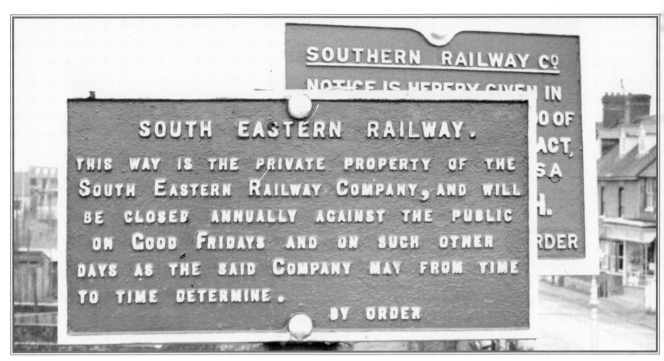

At Paddock Wood, this SER 'Right of Way' cast-iron sign is couched in legal language and clearly takes precedence over the SR sign behind. Each is mounted proudly on an old rail post. A sobering thought is that Charles Dickens, an enthusiastic traveller hereabouts, may once have read the SER sign.

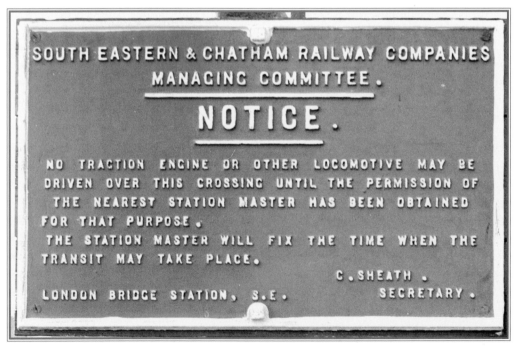

'Traction Engine' signs like this SECR specimen at Chartham have generally been superseded by signs requesting that a telephone call is put through to the signalman – the requisite phone also being supplied. Note the importance of London Bridge, the former Headquarters of the SER – its two-letter postcode could nowadays extend to some four letters and three numerals. Note also that the SECR was two companies managed by a committee.

A cluster of cast-iron signs on a crossing outside Liberty Works, near Merton Abbey. Two posts are concrete and one is wooden. The L&SWR 'beware' sign is the oldest – the 'L', '&' and 'W' were often painted out to leave just 'SR'. Its heavy style of lettering is perpetuated on the Southern 'trespassers' sign on the left.

Lawyers had a field-day when this warning was devised in 1946, since the penalty for defacing this sign near Shepherdswell was greater than the penalty for trespass! This East Kent Railway served the Kent coalfield and the First World War port of Richborough. (The first EKR became the LCDR in 1859.)

A nondescript but delightful 'caution' sign in Nine Elms goods station near the LSWR main line. The letters are studded with 'cats-eyes' for night working, screwed to a wooden board upon a tubular steel post. Three screws are missing, two from the 'S' and one from the 'B'. Who took them?

This SR enamelled name-plate is mounted on simulated bullhead rails but the starting signals are on genuine old rails. The signal-box is SER and the EPB train is BR. The Addiscombe branch opened in 1864 to compete with the LBSCR for Croydon's growing commuter traffic. It was electrified in 1926. In the days of SER steam, there was once a direct service from here to Liverpool Street.

During the 1920s the SR installed platform name-signs of cast concrete, complete with finials. This one at Ventnor also shows the station elevation of 294 feet. Two such signs are evident, together with an SR gantry and a concrete platelayers' hut. The signal-box is of IWR in-house design and the wooden fish van is LBSCR. All are dwarfed by the great natural barrier of St Boniface Down. The emergence of a steam train from the tunnel was sudden and exciting, with the immediate surrender of the single-line token. Note the start of the gradient down through the tunnel.

When stations are downgraded to halts, maintenance of buildings and surrounds becomes less of a priority. Here at Brasted, shrubs have grown large and unkempt, and encroach upon the platform, creeping around the 'barley-sugar' lamp standard and up the station name-posts. The enamelled name-sign is BR, the Sugg Rochester gas lamp with swan-neck is SR, and the heavy canopy and valance are of SER vintage. A push-pull train of SECR stock approaches from the Westerham direction.

Weymouth's gas lamps were similar to Brasted's (opposite) but with different swan-necks. The four-wheel barrows are of the type commonly used for mailbags. The young enthusiast is admiring BR standard class 4 No. 76018. The three leading coaches are SR Maunsell, SR Bulleid and BR Mark 1.

Whitened letters and numerals stand out on a concrete gradient post at the Sydenham end of Penge tunnel. The signal equipment includes the telephone box, an SR starter on an LCDR post, and a distant-repeater for the tunnel ahead. A new colour-light post and terminal boxes are under construction. A service hut stands beyond, almost buried like a bunker.

The front top panel of this SER oil lantern has the station name in white upon a dark background. There are air vents top and bottom, a finial on the top cowl and fancy ironwork at the top corners. The waist is fairly narrow. A bracket-mounted version can be seen on page 11.

A BR enamelled station name-totem is mounted on this LCDR straight-fluted standard at Bearsted & Thurnham on the Ashford West line. The 'gentlemen' sign beyond is SR. The oil lantern is narrow-waisted and neat-looking. Note the iron railings, heavy platform canopy and deep LCDR valance.

Two types of LBSCR oil lantern could be found at Cowden. The first is suspended through its chimney from a swan-neck secured to the platform shelter. The lamp is squatter and less ornate than that at Cliffe, and the overhang is more pronounced. The far lamp is similar to that at Grange Road (overleaf).

Two LSWR spiral-fluted lamp standards at Verwood, together with a station nameboard with wooden cut-out letters. The oil lanterns are tall with a wide waist; the near one has shades. The weather-boarded porter's hut and small signal-box are quaint, and rather overshadowed by the Albion Hotel beyond.

The evening sunlight is perfect to bring out the straight fluting and ornamentation of this LBSCR standard at Grange Road. The oil burner is missing but the ladder is in place. The lantern is plain with a wide waist and a pronounced overhang. The face has a ventilation gap near the top and is half-frosted. The concrete loading gauge beyond is SR.

This tall LSWR unfluted lamp standard at Salisbury is highly ornamented at the cradle. It may once have carried a gas lamp. The crude 'inverted saucer' electric lamp is from the earliest period of electrification. Note the 'watering' stop-sign, the BTC enamelled sign and the SR concrete hut.

The SR adopted the LSWR's spiral-fluted lamp standard. This example at Sevenoaks carries EMU stop-signs, loudspeakers, associated electric wires and two designs of gas lamp – SR 'art deco' on the left and an earlier Sugg Rochester on the right. A nice finishing touch is the small central finial.

An SR steel-reinforced concrete standard in 'art deco' style at Ashford, Kent, carrying a spar for loudspeakers together with speaker wires and a top cable. Electric lamp shades are of late SR hexagonal 'art deco' design, manufactured in one piece instead of with the individual panes as seen at Sevenoaks.

These LBSCR seats at Hayling Island have fewer slats than their LSWR and SER counterparts, and no cross-bracing. The covered van is an SR Maunsell. The train is non-corridor – the LSWR composite has lavatories for the two first-class compartments only. One of the BR coaches is in crimson and cream.

This seat at Sydenham Hill has a cast SER motif and a different arrangement of slats and ironwork compared with the LSWR type seen opposite. How it got onto the LCDR system is anyone's guess! The exclamation on the blackboard is to remind off-peak motormen to stop short EMUs at the 4-car sign.

An SR enamelled name-plate is screwed to this LBSCR seat at Cooksbridge. Waiting for the train, whether for photographing or travelling, could be most pleasant in summer. This is a rare picture of the author in full railwaying gear, taken by his fiancée Marion during an outing to the South Downs.

Pride of the Isle of Wight and a nice piece of PR was this highly varnished platform seat, the 'Best Kept Station' award, seen here in the custody of Shanklin. The slatted seat beyond, with its scrolled ironwork and wooden skids, is LSWR. Note the BR posters promoting Holland, Scotland and motor-rail.

Chapter Five

RAILWAYMEN AT WORK

The steam railway of BR(S) was largely unautomated and labour-intensive. While electrification, track circuitry and power signalling had reduced staffing levels to some extent, these reductions were nothing like the huge cuts that came with the end of steam, the Beeching closures, the centralisation/mechanisation of freight handling, and modern management practices. Railway staffing and working practices had barely changed for a century. In the late 1950s and early '60s we were experiencing Victorian standards of customer attention from railway staff who were generally friendly, helpful, diligent, proud and numerous. The system would be regarded as 'inefficient' by present standards, which is no criticism of the steam railwaymen – they did the job they were required to do.

Our pictorial survey shows ordinary Southern railwaymen at work during the final decade of steam, starting with train crews and progressing through station staff and permanent way gangs to signalmen. Some passengers are also included. As settings for crews, this chapter also incorporates a selection of steam locomotives, with representatives from all three pre-Group companies as well as from the SR, LMS and BR. The oldest are the LBSCR 0–6–0 tanks originating in the 1870s, and the youngest are the standard BR classes built in the 1950s.

Three characteristics emerge from the railwaymen shown. First, a contentedness with their work and a willingness to be photographed, in some cases even with a smile. Second, diligence in their work, whether driving an express, shunting, breaking coal, collecting the tablet, pushing a trolley, heaving a tool or simply carrying a bucket. Thirdly, attentiveness as they kept a wary eye on the author – was he endangering himself or interfering with the smooth running of the railway? Although the author carried a BR(S) permit for lineside photography in the non-electrified areas, railway staff nevertheless kept a watchful eye on such visitors – what we would nowadays call 'duty of care'.

To meet such railwaymen was a privilege. One did not interrupt those who were busy, but in rural areas in particular, there were quiet periods between trains when crews, booking clerks, signalmen and gangers would welcome a conversation, which was generally two-way, covering the experiences and interests of both the author and the railwaymen. Most sensed that their way of life was coming to an end and appreciated the efforts of private individuals to record for posterity their historic place in the scheme of things. This chapter is a tribute to all the friendly railwaymen whom the author met.

See also details in other chapters: engine crew, pp. ii, viii, 40, 116, 117; yardmen, pp. 43, 123; trackmen, pp. 66, 102; stationmen, pp. 11, 12, 35; signalmen, p. viii; passengers, pp. 9, 14, 22, 75, 79.

Cab Posture No. 1 – and a smile from a crewman of SECR 0–4–4 class H tank No. 31161 as it departs East Grinstead for Three Bridges. Harry Wainwright introduced this class in 1904 for suburban passenger duty. The hybrid push-pull set comprises an LBSCR composite and an SECR third with cab end.

Cab Posture No. 2 – with two cheeky young faces leaning out of a BR coach at Langston. Crewmen always looked too big for the 'Terrier' tanks. This was originally LBSCR No. 61 *Sutton*, built in 1875. The blank flange on the side-tank was once fitted with a condensing pipe for operation on the East London line.

Cab Posture No. 3 features LSWR 0–4–4 class M7 tank No. 30033 on yard duty at Eastleigh. Designed by Dugald Drummond, the class was introduced in 1897 for suburban passenger duty. Its 'angularity' was enhanced by the flush side to the tank and cab, and by the sand boxes over the leading splashers.

Cab Posture No. 4 features LBSCR 0–6–0 class E1 tank No. 32694 on ash duty at Fratton MPD. The class was introduced in 1874 for freight. Stroudley characteristics include the flattish roof with central bulge, round-topped side-tanks, cab-mounted brake-pump and a tool box at the rear.

Cab posture No. 5 features SR 4–6–0 'King Arthur' class No. 30769 *Sir Balan*, awaiting the green flag at Canterbury East with a semi-fast to Victoria. Two SR signs guard the barrow crossing, together with a new BR sign – 'Don't touch conductor rail' – serving as a valediction to steam.

Cab posture No. 6 features LBSCR 0–6–0 class C2X No. 32535 shunting coal wagons at Grange Road. D.E. Marsh introduced the class in 1908 as rebuilds of Robert Billington's class C2 of 1893 vintage. The goods brake and loading gauge are both SR. Note the cluster of coaling tools on the tender.

Open Cab No. 1 features SECR 0–6–0 class C No. 31268, running tender-first from Cranbrook to Hawkhurst with a pick-up goods. The safety valve is blowing and eyes are on the pressure gauge. Designed by Harry Wainwright, the class was introduced in 1900. The tenders were exceptionally long.

Open Cab No. 2 features 'King Arthur' class 4–6–0 No. 30800 *Sir Meleaus de Lile*, running light, tender-first to Dover Marine. There is plenty of room for the crew of four, with good rearward vision over the bunker. Robert Urie's class N15 was introduced by the LSWR in 1918 and was further developed by the SR.

The cab of standard 2–6–0 class 4 No. 76012 is enclosed by the high bulkhead of the tender. The coal bunker is tall but narrow, with rearward vision for the crew through the small rear-windows. Breaking the larger lumps of coal was a duty for this fireman at Portsmouth & Southsea terminus. A pair of corrugated SR starting signals stand beyond, together with a tall yard lamp – an early electric type mounted on an SR concrete post.

Unless there were parcels or mailbags to load, the guard could delay opening his door until the train was nearly ready to depart. Such was the scene at Faversham, with water-filling in progress. Standard 4–6–0 class 4 No. 75066 was allocated a high-rave tender (compare with previous picture).

Two drivers and a fireman during a crew change at Basingstoke. The topic of conversation was no doubt the running of 'Battle of Britain' class Pacific No. 34064 *Fighter Command*, heading a Down train in 1963. The air-smoothed casing looks immaculate (compared with No. 75066 above).

Ivatt 2–6–2 tank No. 41317 takes water at Calstock before continuing its journey onto Dartmoor. Three railwaymen are at work in the autumn sunshine of 1959: the guard emerging from his Maunsell compartment; the fireman directing the water hose; and the driver operating the valve chain. Note the leather window-strap, the standard method for over a century to operate and set carriage windows.

This guard at Portsmouth & Southsea high-level is smartly turned out in dark blue serge and with a wide-topped peaked hat. After depositing a piece of 'luggage in advance', the green flag is waved for his EMU to proceed to Waterloo. The Maunsell 4-COR stock was introduced in 1937 when the Portsmouth Direct line was electrified. With their blind eye and flapping gangways, they were affectionately known as 'Nelsons'.

Serge and peaked caps were also worn by motormen in the relative cleanliness and comfort of EMU driving cabs. This motorman emerges from the Redhill shuttle at Reigate, the limit of electrification on the SER's Dorking line. Built in the 1930s, the 2-BIL stock had corridors and lavatories but no gangways.

A guard's door is opened at Bere Alston on a train from Plymouth. Built in 1933, Maunsell brake-third No. 3800 was always part of set No. 241: originally four coaches long; then six coaches in 1938 for the Bournemouth dining service; then three coaches in the mid-1950s until withdrawal in 1962 (ref. 7.5). Sadly, the guard's service history is not on record.

The humble porter was commonplace on the steam railway. At Redhill, he witnesses the arrival of class N Mogul No. 31869. The ornate canopy valance is SER. The SR starting signals have mechanical route indicators for the three Down lines, to Tonbridge, Brighton and Guildford respectively.

This porter or labourer at Sheerness-on-Sea displays his waistcoat buttons. His attention is drawn by the squeal of flanges on check-rails as a Wainwright 0–6–0 class 'C' reverses onto the run-round loop. The platforms and canopy are LCDR, the coach is LSWR and the locomotive is SECR.

A porter wheels his barrow alongside a pile of mailbags at Portsmouth & Southsea high-level. Meanwhile, a child bids farewell to an elderly relative on an EMU bound for Waterloo. Note the LSWR seats, also the SR concrete standard with 'art deco' brackets and lamps. All public railways on Portsea Island were joint LBSCR/LSWR.

Station-masters' hats were large and distinguished with gold braid on the peak. Porters' hats were floppy with small peaks. Drivers' caps were weather-resistant and spongeable. 'Schools' class 4–4–0 No. 30903 *Charterhouse* stands at Portsmouth & Southsea terminus with a smart train of Bulleid stock. Note the great span of the cantilevered canopy.

A ten-pronged fork is used for a spot of weeding at Shanklin, just beyond the range of the chemical weed-killing train. Dominating the scene are the BR enamelled sign and the SR rail-built post with Starting and Warning signals. The latter was no doubt deemed necessary for shunting and running round on the severe grades to either end of the station – a reminder to pin down brakes on loose wagons.

Urban railway workers sometimes scurried around like mice. Dwarfed by the new BR signal-box at Cannon Street, a cleaner or labourer carries a bucket on the tight curve to Borough Market junction.

In the electrified areas, permanent way gangs are apparently immune to shock. Here they are working at the start of the ramp to Portsmouth & Southsea high-level. To the right are the terminal platforms. To the left are EMU service sidings, once the site of Greetham Street goods depot.

This Lyme Regis signalman looks in harmony with his small LSWR signal-box. It housed a ground-frame and had an elaborate chimney vent. Note also the fire buckets and oil can. The corridor coaches beyond are in the bay siding, stored for a return through-working to Waterloo.

Opposite: Photographed from the footbridge, Uckfield's elderly signalman operates the wheel of the SR crossing gates from the convenience of his signal-box. This Saxby & Farmer box opened in 1882. Unlike other LBSCR boxes of this type, the top-lights are panelled instead of glazed. Note the row of dowels for extra stability of the sliding side-window.

At Sandown, all eyes are upon the arrival of a commuting train to Ryde. Centre-stage, the signalman is about to collect the token and return to his elevated box, whose door stands open. Note the clock and destination boards – only one was needed after the withdrawal of Newport services from the far platform.

At Tower Hill, a signalman stands ready to exchange the tablet for single-line working on the North Cornwall line. This early train is bound for Exeter, headed by Bulleid light Pacific No. 34104 *Bere Alston*. The oil-lamps and barrow are LSWR. The enamelled 'gents' and concrete name-sign are SR.

A conversation between West Grinstead's signalman and the driver of class M7 tank No. 30049. The goods yard looks busy, with a long siding of coal wagons and at least four horse-boxes serving the dock. Note the pointwork arrangement, which prevented direct access to sidings from the running lines.

One of the MPD roads at Callington was used for dry storage of loco coal. This duty loco was therefore 'stabled' by the water column. A crewman approaches LMS 2–6–2 class 2 tank No. 41302 while the signalman carries the token. The first train of the day will shortly depart to Bere Alston. See page 136 for Cheap Market Tickets from this station. They were a bargain!

Chapter Six

LINES, TRACK AND CIVIL WORKS

The Southern had the world's first passenger steam railway, the Canterbury & Whitstable, which opened in 1830 and was followed by the Bodmin & Wadebridge line in 1834. London's first passenger railway was the London & Greenwich, which opened in 1836. This was constructed on a viaduct of 878 brick arches to avoid the marshes of Bermondsey and Deptford. Viaducts proved to be most suitable for running through urban developments, requiring the narrowest of widths and allowing roads and footways to pass beneath. This set the standard for many urban railways around the world. Elevated stations could be awkward, however, with exposed, draughty platforms, as seen in Chapter One.

The London & Southampton line opened in 1838 with a terminus at Nine Elms, later extended by viaduct to Waterloo. London's earliest terminus, London Bridge, was expanded progressively to accommodate trains not only from Greenwich but from new railways – the London & Croydon (1839), the London & Brighton (1841) and the South Eastern (1842). They shared the line through Brockley cutting to Croydon, then through cuttings and tunnels to Redhill where the SER took a dog-leg due east to Folkestone. This SER main line was as level and straight as possible – a feature of other early railways including the London & Southampton.

As confidence grew in civil engineering and as locomotives became more powerful, subsequent lines took more tortuous routes through hilly country, incorporating severe gradients, tunnels and viaducts. The LSWR main line to Exeter became known as the 'switchback', while the LCDR went up, down and through the North Downs for most of its length. The Croydon to Brighton main line was lightly graded but major civil works were unavoidable, crossing the North Downs, High Weald and South Downs. The Balcombe viaduct across the Ouse Valley, with Italianate pavilions at either end, was engineered in brick and stone by John Rastick, with architecture by David Mocatta. It is possibly the finest ever built (ref. 1.3).

The Southern inherited many fine civil structures. Long, low viaducts in stone, brick and steel crossed estuaries and harbours such as Folkestone, Bursledon, Fareham, Barnstaple and the Tavy, while tall inland viaducts could be found at Foord (brick), Eynsford (brick and stone), London Road, Brighton (curved in brick), Calstock (concrete blocks), Cannington (concrete cast *in situ*) and Meldon (steel trestles). There were, of course, thousands of ordinary bridges in steel and brick, both over and beneath the railway, together with numerous tunnels. The Civil Engineering Department would inspect all such structures regularly and carry out repairs and maintenance as necessary. Many bridges had been strengthened to accommodate ever-greater locomotive axle loads, particularly on the LCDR whose lines had been built at rock-bottom cost.

All three principal pre-Group companies built complex suburban networks. These were subsequently inter-connected and electrified to become the largest integrated commuting system in the world. This awesome giant was not without its problems, suffering overcrowding during the twice-daily rush-hours and under-use at other times.

Although the railway promoted commuting from the leafy suburbs, such traffic may never have been economic. It is subsidised to this day.

The 'railway mania' extended to southern provincial towns and rural areas. Numerous secondary and branch lines were built, in many cases uneconomic but often deemed necessary in order to keep a rival company at bay. Duplicate services were provided and competition was both intense and crippling. Rationalisation of lines and services followed the SECR merger of 1899, the Southern grouping of 1923 and Nationalisation in 1948. There was a steady trickle of rural line closures, culminating in the Beeching tidal wave from the mid-1960s. All the Southern main lines remained intact, however, during the reign of BR steam.

Our pictures show contrasts between the busy multi-track lines in London and the tranquillity of the rural branch. Different types of track are illustrated, together with a selection of tunnels, bridges and viaducts. (The usual definition of a railway viaduct is a bridge of four or more arches.) All the lines and structures shown are pre-Group, a tribute to the golden age of railway construction. Some of the rural track is original (late Victorian), but not on busy lines where it was renewed regularly due to wear.

Reference
6.1 Smith, M., *British Railway Bridges & Viaducts*, Ian Allan, 1994.

See also details in other chapters: track, pp. ii, 2, 12, 16, 31, 41, 43, 52, 65, 125; pointwork, pp. 11, 33, 39, 47, 49, 61, 73, 95, 99, 123; bridges, pp. 8, 12, 14, 15, 23, 27; tunnels, pp. 21, 35, 64, 66, 73.

This remarkable ballast-washing machine was photographed in the lower yard at East Grinstead in July 1959. The purpose of ballast cleaning was to ensure good drainage of the track. The heaps of earthenware drain-pipes between the grassy tracks give the scene a rather unnatural appearance.

Cannon Street's complex pointwork stretches the full width of the Thames. Track maintenance is in progress during the middle of the day when no services are scheduled. This was the SER's City terminus, opening in 1866. Scaffolding is being erected to dismantle the roof, which was severely damaged during the war. Extensive bomb damage is also evident beyond the bridge.

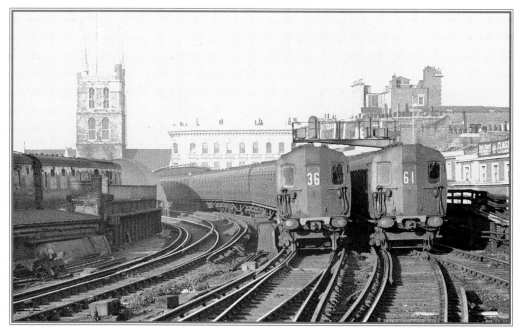

A notorious SER bottle-neck was between London Bridge and Borough Market junction, where six tracks narrowed into four. Two trains of EPB stock are neck-and-neck, bound respectively for Addiscombe (36) and Dartford via Blackheath and Charlton (61). Southwark Cathedral looms beyond. This costly extension to the City and West End was built to compete with the LCDR.

South of Clapham Junction, eight parallel tracks serve suburbia as well as most of the south coast. The loop line (left) leads to the LSWR milk platform. The double junction (right) leads to the West London line. The stubs of former LBSCR overhead electric gantries are embedded in the wall on the right. An Oxted steam train to Victoria is passing a stopping 4-SUB service from Waterloo.

By contrast, this single-track in North Devon served the local china clay industry. It was one of the few new lines built by the SR, and opened in 1925. Engineered by Colonel Stephens, it was a light railway with some tight curves. A mixed passenger-freight train from Torrington is seen near Watergate halt.

Opposite: This detail from Woldingham shows bullhead double-track with steel spring wedges. A single signal-wire is suspended along the left, alongside a concrete channel recently laid for impending colour-light signalling. Restarting, centre-scene, is a train to Victoria, headed by a standard 2–6–4 tank.

Rail/flange greasers reduce the wear on the outside rails of curves. This example was installed on some new BR track near High Halstow halt. As train wheels pass over the three applicator plates, small quantities of grease are forced onto the flanges. It was a platelayer's task to replenish the pot.

A close-up of concrete sleepers and a footpath crossing near Langston. The crossing is a combination of steel channels and wooden sleepers laid upon long beams. The rails are traditional British bullhead.

Bullhead chairs usually had three bolts. This specimen at Cliffe is dated 1900 and marked SE&CDR, an early version of the abbreviation that became SE&CR. The wedge is wooden and obsolete, superseded by steel spring wedges. A trackman's task was to inspect, replace and tighten wedges by hammer.

A two-bolt chair of the Isle of Wight Railway, dated 1883 and photographed at Merstone on the IWCR.
The chair post-dates the opening of the Newport–Sandown line and may have been laid when the station
became a junction for the Ventnor West branch, which opened in 1900.

Photographed in April 1960 near Horringford, the end is nigh for the IWCR's Sandown line. Dismantled sleepers and rails are neatly laid out, awaiting removal by lorry. This grand, empty landscape scarcely noticed the arrival and closure of the railway. A youthful River Yar flows by regardless!

Where tunnel portals were not in the public eye, ornamentation was deemed unnecessary. Such was the case at Black Boy Road tunnel, on the final descent into Exeter Central. First of its class, 'Merchant Navy' class Pacific No. 35001 *Channel Packet* is seen emerging with the 'Atlantic Coast Express'.

Crystal Palace (high-level) was opened by the LCDR in 1865. The line was built along the ridge (just below), and passengers had access to the Palace by subway. The architecture and finish were imposing, not least that of the tunnel portal with elaborate yellow brickwork, strong columns and some classical stonework.

The LBSCR invested heavily in infrastructure. The 'Inner Circle' country route to Brighton (via Oxted, East Grinstead and Haywards Heath) was built to main line standards with some imposing stone over-bridges. Beneath this elegant arch, north of Horsted Keynes, were stored several miles of condemned wagons, mostly wooden and open, during the late 1950s. The nearside track was disused. But for the intervention of the Second World War, this line would have been electrified.

Opposite: A fine brick viaduct across the Great Stour near Wye, reflecting a century of weathering and knocks from passing boats. Overhead, a Bulleid 0–6–0 class Q1 is shunting goods wagons.

For the Tulse Hill line through Dulwich College Estates, certain bridge ornamentations were stipulated. This iron panel of 1866 bears the shields of Dulwich College (right) and of the LBSCR (left). On the latter can be seen the cross and sword of the City of London as well as the star and crescent of Portsmouth.

One of the tall viaducts on the Southern was at Cannington. Cast in concrete *in situ*, using novel construction techniques, its clean lines remain a memorial to the Lyme Regis branch, which closed in 1965.

Chapter Seven

ROLLING STOCK

The words 'carriage', 'coach' and 'car' are synonymous. In Britain, however, it is conventional to use 'carriage' or 'coach' for locomotive-hauled stock and the American term 'car' for multiple units (EMUs and DMUs). During the 1950s and early 1960s Southern Region enthusiasts could discover a wealth of carriage types spanning over half a century of design and manufacture. A broad guide to identify some of the common main line steam stock from that era is as follows:

Coach Type	Body Construction	Derivation	Some Changes from Predecessor
BR Mark1	All steel	SR Bullied	No beading, no roof strips
SR Bulleid	Timber, steel clad	SR Maunsell	Rounded windows; guard's periscope
SR Maunsell	Timber, steel clad	LSWR 'Ironclad'	Tall flush windows; small duckets
LSWR 'Ironclad'	Timber, steel clad	Original	No panelling; corridors
SECR 'Continental'	Wooden matchboard	Original	No panelling; corridors
Older pre-Group	Wooden panelled	Company styles	Bogies

Working down this list, duties ranged from express to secondary, branch line and 'service vehicle', perhaps ending up in isolated sidings, then as grounded bodies and eventually scrap. A lucky few avoided or postponed being scrapped by being sold or earmarked for preservation, or by being transferred for a new lease of life to the Isle of Wight. One common feature to all on the list was the 'torpedo' roof vent. All the BR and SR coaches had corridors and gangway connections and were readily distinguishable from each other by their windows, sides, roof details, guard's look-outs, etc. There were variations of each type, such as conversions to push-pull and the Maunsell flat-sided stock.

The pre-Group bogie coaches were enchanting, brimming with Edwardian elegance. Most designs had full mahogany or teak panelling and beading, a low roof profile and a prominent guard's look-out. Variations included conversions to push-pull operation. Early twentieth-century rail motors were also converted to push-pull. A guide to the principal pre-Group coaches to be found in BR days is as follows:

Low-roof stock	SECR	LBSCR	LSWR
Roof type	flattened elliptical	arc	flattened elliptical
Gauge width	8 ft or 8 ft 6 in	8 ft	9 ft
Guard's look-out	birdcage	duckets	duckets
Door vent hoods	plain	slatted	slatted
Hand rails	Z shape (usually)	long slender	short straight

High elliptical roof stock	'Continental'	'Balloon'	'Ironclad'
Gauge width	8 ft	8 ft 6 in	9 ft
Guard's look-out	rear windows	rear windows	rear windows
Door vent hoods	plain	plain	plain
Hand rails	long thick	long slender	short straight

The high elliptical coaches were relatively few in number; all had corridors and gangways for toilet and restaurant car access. In contrast, the SR inherited vast quantities of low-roof stock, mostly non-corridor 'sardine cans' for London suburban service. Some non-bogie coaches were retained until the late 1930s for workmen's trains, specials and excursions. The Isle of Wight was a haven for old coaches, with LCDR bogie stock in daily use until the late 1940s and SECR/LBSCR bogie stock until electrification in 1967.

During the 1920s low-roof coaches from all three companies were converted for electric service. The LBSCR and LSWR were pioneers of electrification, and the SR adopted the LSWR's third-rail dc system as standard in preference to the LBSCR's overhead ac system. From the mid-1920s onwards, as electrification programmes were implemented, new electric stock was introduced to the successive designs of Maunsell, Bulleid and BR(S). Coaches were made up into close-coupled EMUs as opposed to the numbered 'Sets' of SR steam stock. The Westinghouse air brake was standard for EMUs and on the Isle of Wight, having a quicker response than the vacuum brakes that were standard on mainland SR steam stock.

The EMU classification '4-SUB' covered many different suburban coach designs, ranging from conversions of wooden stock in the 1920s to the Bulleid all-steel designs of the 1940s. They were non-corridor except that Bulleid introduced the semi-saloon with an offset central gangway. Most had domed roof-ends and were vee-fronted to a greater or lesser degree. In 1951, however, a new suburban EMU was introduced with a square roof-end and flat front, and classified 'EPB' by virtue of Electro-Pneumatic Brakes.

New EMU stock was built for main line electrification in the 1930s. The Brighton system had a range of corridor express units, some with Pullman coaches, together with semi-fast stock with internal corridors but no inter-car gangways. The Portsmouth Direct line was the first with comprehensive thru-train gangways, an arrangement that was repeated for the Kent Coast electrification of 1959 (LCDR) and 1961 (SER). The SER's Hastings line was served by a unique design of flat-sided Diesel Multiple Unit (DMU) from 1957 until electrification in 1986.

In the days of BR steam, there was therefore a rich variety of coach types on the Southern. Coach livery was predominantly Southern green, with the occasional dash of BR 'blood & custard', maroon or suburban red. Although BR(S) was predominantly a passenger railway, there was also a full range of goods wagon types, from the steel designs of BR to the wooden stock of SR and its pre-Group parents. A selection of wagons is included in this chapter, as well as being liberally scattered throughout the book.

References

7.1   Ellis, C.H., *Railway Carriages in the British Isles from 1930 to 1914*, George Allen & Unwin, 1965.

7.2   Jenkinson, D., *British Railway Carriages of the 20th Century*, Vol 1: 1901–22, Patrick Stephens, 1988.

7.3   Kichenside, G.M., *Railway Carriages 1839–1939*, Ian Allan, 1964.

7.4   Gould, D., *Bogie Carriages of the SECR*, The Oakwood Press, 1993.

7.5   Gould, D., *Maunsell's SR Steam Carriage Stock*, The Oakwood Press, 1990.

See also details in other chapters: SECR coaches, pp. 2, 19, 74, 83, 99; LBSCR coach, p. 83; LSWR coaches, pp. 80, 92; SR Maunsell steam, pp. 52, 75, 77, 88, 89, 91, 103; SR Bulleid steam, pp. 41, 44, 75, 93, 97; BR Mark 1, pp. 55, 75; BR non-corridor, pp. 80, 83; Hastings DMU, p. 11; EMU, pp. 40, 47, 50, 61, 65, 72, 90, 91, 93, 95, 102, 103; goods wagons, pp. 13, 32, 33, 34, 35, 38, 40, 41, 42, 43, 73, 80, 85, 99, 103, 109.

In 1905/06 the SECR built eight rail motors (a coach integral with an 0–4–0 tank) but they were under-powered. In 1924 they were converted to two-car push-pull sets with steel panelling. No. 481 served on branches to Bembridge, Gravesend West, Swanley-Sevenoaks and from 1932 to 1959 mostly to Westerham (ref. 7.4). It is seen here at Gravesend Central. Note the SER goods shed, SR lamps, SER seats and the multiplicity of advertisements. The coach with roof piping and a single line of torpedo vents is LSWR.

The ultra-high elliptical roof of the LBSCR's 'balloon' stock. Used from 1905 for prestige boat trains and expresses, plus a few for push-pull duty, they were confined mainly to the LBSCR system. This lavatory brake-third ended its days as an immobile service vehicle at Plymouth Friary.

LSWR 'gate stock' dates from the early 1900s. The first two were built by Drummond as rail motors for the joint LSWR/ LBSCR service to East Southsea. Push-pull set No.373 is photographed at Yeovil Junction in 1959, shortly before withdrawal, on 'the bunk' service to Yeovil Town.

Late Victorian non-bogie passenger stock generally had the low arc roof. Some had loop handles. This LSWR four-compartment first-class body was one of a group occupying the quay opposite Padstow station platform. It must have been grounded after completion of the South Quay in 1910 (see page 44).

A 'birdcage' service vehicle, marked 'Engineers' Dept', in a bay at Hildenborough. It was formerly an SECR
composite brake with lavatories for the central first-class compartments. There were numerous variations of
such stock – the SECR era was a golden one for coach development and experimentation.

In 1921 the LSWR introduced high elliptical roof, steel-sided corridor coaches known as 'Ironclads'.
Produced until 1926, they were the basis of the SR's subsequent coach designs under Maunsell. Push-pull set
No. 383, built in 1925, is seen at Yeovil Junction. The SR ground-signal is for exiting sidings.

A condemned service vehicle in a Ramsgate siding, marked 'CWE' for Carriage & Wagon Examiner. It was formerly an SECR brake-third, part of a 'Trio C' set that broke with tradition in 1915 by omitting the 'birdcage' and beading. Note the truss rods with turnbuckle for pulling the chassis into shape.

Maunsell Restriction 0 (8 ft) flat-sided stock was built for service through the narrow tunnels south of Tonbridge. Unlike the parent 9 ft stock, there were no guards' duckets (see page 91). A three-car set passes Redgate Mill Junction, en route to Uckfield, Lewes and Brighton, behind a standard 2–6–4 tank. The timber S&F signal-box is of the same type as at Oxted (see page viii).

The 'Brighton Belle' was the Southern's most prestigious EMU service. Introduced in 1932, there were
three 5-BEL units comprising five Pullman cars of all-steel construction. Resplendent in cream and brown
livery, unit No. 3053 coasts through Selhurst in 1958, heading a Down service from Victoria.

The semi-fast 2-BIL units were introduced in 1937 when electrification reached Portsmouth and Reading.
Coaches had corridors and lavatories but no gangways. Unit 2124 approaches Lewes in the delightful setting
of the former St Oswald's Priory. The distant signals are for the junction for Seaford. Journeys in such trains
along the south coast always felt comfortable, secure and civilised.

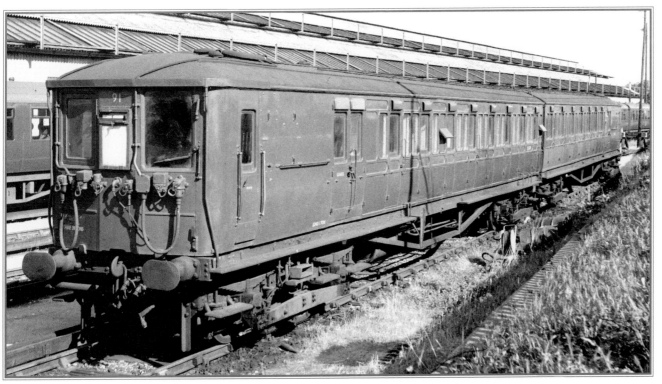

LBSCR coaches were the last survivors of the pre-Group steam stock conversions of the mid-1920s. Built as 3-SUB units, they were later enlarged to hybrid 4-SUB units by the addition of a wider Bulleid coach. Some motor coaches subsequently became two-car de-icing units, including No. 91 seen here at Fratton in 1958. The low arc roof is disguised by its domed end.

Oliver Bulleid's post-war all-steel 4-SUB units were modernistic with rounded windows. This pair is in sidings at Crystal Palace (low-level), outside the wall of the great station. Unit 4295 was all-new, built in 1949. Unit 4691 had a new body upon a pre-Group underframe, put together during 1951–6.

The 2-NOL units were conversions of LSWR steam stock. The standard SR cab ends are the same as for the LBSCR conversions (see previous page), the driver's window being larger than the opening window. Unit 1844 rests in the service sidings at Selhurst depot. Note the short whistle (top right).

In 1949 the Southern built a pair of experimental four-coach double-deck units, intended to ease the overcrowding on Eastern Section commuter trains. Loading times were excessive, however, and trains were instead increased to ten cars. 4-DD unit 4002 is seen here at London Bridge.

The very first Bulleid 4-SUB units, built in 1941, were the last with domed roof ends and the last with stencil-type headcodes – in this case 94 for Victoria to Coulsdon North. Unit 4108 is at Clapham Junction, showing buffers, screw-coupling, lamp irons and brake/electrical/ control connectors.

A contrast of EMU cab ends at London Bridge terminus: unit 5754 is a 2-EPB built in the 1950s with a flat front and square roof end; unit 4321 is a 4-SUB built in 1925, all-new but retaining the domed roof end and pronounced vee front inherited from the original LSWR motor coaches of 1915.

Service vehicle No. DS 3185 in a siding at Newport, Isle of Wight. It was formerly an LCDR four-wheel passenger brake van but steel cladding has been applied more recently to cover the ageing wood panelling. Beyond are a pair of IWCR water tanks on LSWR frames, used for weed killing (ref. 0.8). Newport station stands beyond, with the 'Freshwater' yard on the right.

Service vehicle No. DS1522 rests in a dilapidated state in a siding at Exeter Central. It was formerly an SER/SECR six-wheel passenger brake van boasting end windows, three pairs of doors, and duckets at either end. Another version had central duckets plus birdcage, but no sliding doors or end windows.

The Isle of Wight is renowned for longevity. This beach hut at St Helens was formerly an LBSCR four-wheel goods brake van from the Stroudley era (1870–89), having no verandah. An earlier version had a 'birdcage' look-out or 'lantern'. Pictured in 1960, the body looks in remarkably good condition. Other beach huts nearby included a grounded rake of Metropolitan Railway bogie coaches.

Loose shunting in the goods yard at Lyme Regis, with the shunter ready to apply the brake to a Maunsell 12 ton wooden van. Other wagons are a mix of BR 16 ton all-steel mineral and BR 12 ton covered. Note the engine shed, double-slip point, point levers and yard lamp with permanent ladder.

LSWR goods brake vans had three sections – a verandah, a guard's compartment and a large goods compartment. This allowed them to pick up and deliver light goods at stations 'on the road', hence their common name 'road van'. No. S548 is photographed at Ventnor, alongside a five-plank 10 ton open wagon.

The SR's 25 ton goods brake had a distinctive body, shorter than its chassis. This one is at Downton with a container wagon. Note the LSWR seat, stretcher cupboard, clock, canopy brackets, and disused signal-box.

A distant Kingscote signal stands with tapered post and faded bands,
A relic of the Brighton years – is that a Stroudley tank one hears?
The line through Horsted Keynes could boast an 'Inner Circle' to the coast,
Where once those green remembered trains brought motion, steam and whistle-strains.
Ancient wagons, bullhead track – all condemned, there's no way back –
And yet, I sense a 'Bluebell' train will one day pass this way again.

TICKETS, LABELS AND NOTICES

The author's railway interests were catholic, encompassing not only photography, history, modelling and hard relics, but also 'ephemera' – those tickets, labels, leaflets and other pieces of paper intended for a short life. After tramping between stations to photograph the steam railway, one of the great pleasures was to arrive at a country station and to meet the staff. A platform ticket would be purchased, then one would enquire what old tickets might be in the racks. Most office staff would respond with spirit, perusing their ticket stock for low numbers and for those that had faded to brown around the edges. Sometimes the author was invited to browse for himself, not only for tickets but for labels and other ancient treasures. The constraint was usually money – the author was a student with little spare cash, and he therefore tended to buy cheap tickets to nearby destinations. Occasionally, a more expensive ticket might be purchased and used to a point near his next destination, taking care not to have to hand it in, of course. Over the years a huge collection was built up, mostly of BR(S) tickets and labels but including many vintage SR and pre-Group. The remote, little-used stations had the best collections of old tickets; most of them are now closed, of course. An objective never quite completed was to buy a platform ticket from every Southern station.

The illustrations show most of the ticket types still purchasable into the 1960s. The small luggage labels show a range of printing styles, printing dates and destinations, including some strange names that have since changed. Some larger parcels labels are included, also some wagon consignment cards. A selection of pre-Group notices and letters show different styles of letter-heads and presentation. Two letters about SECR electric lighting were rescued during the author's apprenticeship at Bankside Power Station, when archives were being thrown out; one is dated 1905 and the other 3 January 1923, over-stamped SR, just two days after the Grouping.

The BR 'excursion' leaflet to Allhallows is typical of thousands that adorned booking hall racks, indicative of the trouble that planners and publicity staff went to in order to maximise passenger revenue. There are two samples of art-work – one from an SR map of 1929 and one for the 'Golden Arrow' service for 1958/9.

Reference

8.1   Fairchild, G. and Wootton, P., *Railway & Tramway Tickets*, Ian Allan, 1987.

See also large posters on the stations in Chapter One and on pages 81, 98 and 114 .

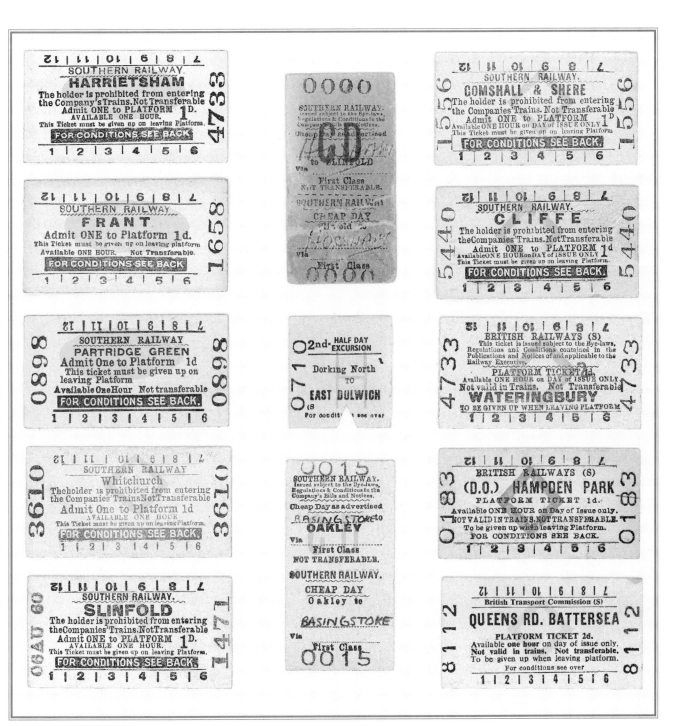

A selection of Platform tickets. The earliest SR style was inherited from the pre-Group companies, having a red oval upon a white ground. The SR then introduced its own design, white with a red diamond. This was perpetuated by BR, headed *British Railways* for some years, then with the more familiar *British Transport Commission*. The two SR 1st Class Cheap Day Returns have low numbers, respectively 0000 from Slinfold and 0015 from Oakley. By contrast, BR had sold 710 Half Day Excursions from East Dulwich to Dorking North, this batch being no more than eleven years old.

A selection of SR 3rd Class Singles (left) in dark green, although Sharnal Street has faded almost to white. A
BR 2nd Class Single is included for comparison. The SR 1st Class Singles (right) are white, in various stages
of fading to yellow. The Hawkhurst blank is particularly prized because it has not been filled in and is
undated – the author was trusted not to use it for a free ride to Padstow! The Day Return tickets are rare,
two of them for sports clubs and one for Brixton dwellers seeking a day out in the countryside.

A selection of special SR tickets (left) for Parking, Child and HM Forces on Leave. The SR Returns (centre) have low numbers, especially the Cooksbridge blank, only the sixteenth to be issued in some four decades. The BR bicycle return (centre) is red and the two Parking tickets (top) are blue, respectively for a motor car and a motor cycle. Note that the BR Returns (right) are in 'landscape' instead of the 'portrait' orientation of the SR and early BR. The Gunnislake 1st Class blank is actually Western Region, following changes in the 1950s to the BR regional boundaries. It is numbered 000 – although not filled in, it has been cancelled by pen and dated 5 SEP 59. Oh, to re-live some of those happy journeys!

London Brighton and South Coast Railway.

Partridge Green to

Isfield

London Brighton & South Coast Railway.

Chelsea to

New Croydon

London Brighton and South Coast Railway.

Ford Junction to

Newick & Chailey

Hither Green

London and South Western Ry.
787

From PADSTOW

TO

WEST Bournemouth

Folkestone
CENTRAL

London and South Western Ry.
787

From _____

TO

RYDE

Via PORTSMOUTH.

London and South Western Ry.
787

From _____

TO

Kensington High St.

Via _____

A selection of pre-Group luggage labels (slightly reduced in size) to specific stations. Those without a company name are SECR. All are white except Ryde, which is mauve. Every station had a paste-pot for affixing such labels. Kensington High Street is a reminder that a parcels service was once offered on what is now the London Underground. Only the LBSCR printed both the departure and destination stations. Newick & Chailey was on the Bluebell line, Chelsea was on the West London line and New Croydon was superseded by East Croydon in 1909.

SOUTHERN RAILWAY.
(12/24)   Stock
TO   787
EASTBOURNE
(Via COSHAM and HAVANT)

SOUTHERN RAILWAY.
(6/36)   Stock
TO   787
COWES

SOUTHERN RAILWAY.
(3/25)   Stock
TO   787
OAKLEY

SOUTHERN RAILWAY.
(7/39)   Stock
TO   787
PADDINGTON

SOUTHERN RAILWAY.
(2/26)   Stock
TO   787
DEAL

SOUTHERN RAILWAY.
(9/43)   Stock
TO   787
WADEBRIDGE

SOUTHERN RAILWAY.
(8/26)   Stock
TO   787
WHITSTABLE HARBOUR

SOUTHERN RAILWAY.
(2/46) 24M   Stock
TO   787
POOLE

SOUTHERN RAILWAY.
(7/31)   Stock
TO   787
HOLBORN VIADUCT

SOUTHERN RAILWAY
(4/47) 6M   Stock
TO   787
OXTED

A selection of SR luggage labels (slightly reduced in size) to specific stations, in date order and showing a variety of fonts. All are white, fading to light brown. The general design is clearly inherited from the LSWR (see opposite) but with the 'From' space omitted. Whitstable Harbour was on the world's first passenger railway, opening in 1830, closing to passengers in 1930 and to all traffic in 1952. Other stations that have since closed are Oakley, Holborn Viaduct, Cowes and Wadebridge.

A selection of less specific SR luggage labels (full size), dated 1925 to 1947. The ground is white for all labels except deep pink for the 'L&NER', buff for the 'LM&SR', light mauve for the 'Excessed' and two blue stripes for the BR 'TCF' (To be Called For). All lettering is black except on the 'To Pay' and 'Delivery NOT Included' labels, which are red.

$\left(\frac{5}{37}\right)$ **SOUTHERN RAILWAY.** $\left(\frac{\text{Stock}}{746\,\text{V}}\right)$ $\frac{}{4/26}$

EXPLOSIVES

PLACE AS FAR
AS PRACTICABLE
FROM ENGINE,
BRAKE-VAN and
VEHICLES
LABELLED
"INFLAMMABLE."

DATE_____19___ TRAIN_____

FROM_____

TO_____

VIA_____ Coy._____

SIDING_____

Owner and No. of Wagon_____

Consignee_____

SHUNT
WITH
GREAT
CARE.

LOAD and UNLOAD
OUTSIDE
GOODS SHEDS.

This label to be used for GUNPOWDER and all other EXPLOSIVES.

$\left(\frac{8}{27}\right)$ **SOUTHERN RAILWAY.** $\left(\frac{\text{Stock.}}{746\,\text{B}}\right)$ $\frac{}{6/27}$

From_____
TO_____
VIA_____

and L. M. & S. Ry.

(L. & N. W.)

Consignee_____
Date_____
Wagon No._____
Total Sheets in use_____

$\left(\frac{8}{29}\right)$ **SOUTHERN RAILWAY.** $\left(\frac{\text{Stock}}{746\,\text{A}}\right)$ $\frac{}{6/27}$

From_____
TO_____
VIA_____

and L. M. & S. Ry.

(MIDLAND)

Consignee_____
Date_____
Wagon No._____
Total Sheets in use_____

These SR wagon consignment cards (reduced in size) were acquired at Sharnal Street where there were sidings to connect with the Chattenden Naval Tramway. This carried explosives on a wandering, rural route to Upnor Hard, opposite the Royal Naval Dockyard at Chatham. Such humble pieces of card therefore contributed in a small way to the naval battles of the Second World War.

SOUTHERN RAILWAY. (⅟₇)   Stock (890)

EGGS
WITH CARE.

SOUTHERN RAILWAY (⅟₃₆)   Stock 27 N 2/35

LIVE
STOCK

SOUTHERN RAILWAY. (⅟₁₆)   Stock 87 Y

FRUIT, VEGETABLES,
AND MARKET GOODS.
IMMEDIATE.

From _____
To _____

_____ Railway,

Via _____ Date _____ 19

Owner and No. of Wagon _____

Owner and No. of Sheets and Under Sheets _____

See other side for particulars of contents and Consignees' names.

For		Description and No. of Packages.							
Name	Market	Sieves	Halves	Qrs.	Maunds	Hampers	Sacks	Bags	Crates

SOUTHERN RAILWAY. (⅟₄₅)   Stock 87 O 8/36

DELIVERED LUGGAGE.

From _____

To _____ Station.

_____ Railway,

via _____

Excess charge **to pay** _____

ONE OF THESE LABELS TO BE
AFFIXED TO EACH PACKAGE.

No. of Pack-ages.	No. of Passengers.	
	First Class.	Third Class.

SOUTHERN RAILWAY.   Stock (39 N) 1/36

FRAGILE
WITH CARE.

(Stock 39.P)

SOUTHERN RAILWAY

INSURED

(12)/46

London Brighton & South Coast Railway.

396 (841A)

REFER HERETO

DEPARTMENT.

_____ Station,

IN YOUR REPLY

_____ 192

APPLICATION FOR CHARGES.

SIR,

_____

I am referred to you for charges on above goods, which

we are unable to obtain for the reason_____

I shall be obliged for your early remittance, or in the event of your having an account with this Company authority to place this amount to debit.

Collection ...   .

Carriage   ...   .

Delivery   ...   .

Paid on   ...   .

Yours obediently,

_____

[W. & S. Ltd.]

The 'Insured' label (*above*) is yellow. The 'Fragile', 'Eggs' and 'Live Stock' labels (*opposite*) are deep red. The 'Delivered Luggage' is pink and the 'Fruit & Veg' label is buff (both sides are shown). All five labels are reproduced to a smaller size but the LBSCR notice is full size. Overleaf, the PD&SWJR notice is full size; the LSWR is slightly reduced.

Note the different fonts of 'Southern Railway'. The pre-Group letterheads which follow also have contrasting styles, from the LBSCR Gothic to the plain LSWR and the delightful SECR copperplate.

PLYMOUTH, DEVONPORT AND SOUTH WESTERN JUNCTION RAILWAY.

(Bere Alston and Callington Line.)

CHEAP

MARKET TICKETS

TO

Plymouth & Devonport

WILL BE ISSUED

THURSDAYS & SATURDAYS,

AS UNDER :—

	A.M.	A.M.	FARES:
Callington Road	7.23	9.50	3rd Class Return from any Station TO
Stoke Climsland	7.32	9.57	Devonport 1/8
Latchley - - -	7.39	10.3	Plymouth 1/10
Gunnislake - -	7.51	10.13	(North Rd.)
Calstock - - -	8.8	10.28	Plymouth 2/- (Friary)

Available for return by any Train on the day of issue only.

Children under Three Years of Age, Free; Three and under Twelve, Half-fares.

The Tickets are not transferable, and are subject to the conditions published in the Company's Time Tables and Bills, and in the General Notice containing the conditions on which Tickets are issued to Passengers. Attention is particularly directed to the conditions limiting the availability of Cheap Tickets.

Passengers travelling without personal luggage with these Cheap Market Tickets may carry with them 60 lbs. of marketing goods free of charge (at their own risk), all excess over that weight will be charged for.

February, 1908.   (*By order*) **J. W. BURCHELL,** *Secretary*

BRADBURY, AGNEW, & CO. LD., PRINTERS, LONDON AND TONBRIDGE.   (4211-2-08.)

London and South Western Railway.

W 205

OFFICE OF SUPERINTENDENT OF THE LINE,
WATERLOO STATION, S.E. 1.

Circular No. 897.   *27th August*, 1921.

Instructions to Station Masters and all others concerned.

Conveyance of Parcels and Miscellaneous Traffic.

Commencing on Monday, the 29th instant, the transfer of Parcels and Miscellaneous traffic across London will be accelerated by the withdrawal of the limited rail services and the substitution therefor of Road transfer services as follows :—

To Euston For L. & N. W. R.	To St. Pancras For Midland Rly.	To King's Cross For G. N. R.
Waterloo, depart 12 0 midnight (not Saturdays) 2 30 a.m. 5 0 ,, 7 45 ,, 10 0 ,, 10 15 ,, 1 30 p.m. 1 45 ,, 4 45 ,, 7 0 ,, 7 30 ,, 10 30 ,, (not Saturdays)	Waterloo, depart 3 30 a.m. 9 0 ,, 2 0 p.m. 3 45 ,, 10 0 ,,	Waterloo, depart 2 30 a.m. 6 0 ,, (not Mondays) 9 0 a.m. 12 45 p.m. 5 30 ,, 10 0 ,,

To Marylebone For G. C. R.	To Liverpool Street For G. E. R.	To Paddington For G. W. R.
Waterloo, depart 9 0 a.m. 6 30 p.m.	Waterloo, depart 1 0 a.m. 10 15 ,, 3 15 p.m. (not Saturdays) 7 15 p.m. 9 45 ,, 11 45 ,, (not Saturdays)	Waterloo, depart 7 30 a.m. 7 0 p.m.

[OVER

21816

South Eastern and Chatham Railway.

Electrical Department.

Chief Engineer and Superintendent's Office.

Tonbridge.

W. LEONARD,
ENGINEER & SUPERINTENDENT.

Refer hereto in your reply:-

4th November 1905

F. Bayley Esq

    Engineer

    The City of LondonnElectric Lighting Co
               Bankside. London   S.E.

Dear Sir,

          Lighting of <u>Holborn Snow Hill</u>,Ludgate Hill & St Pauls
                     Route of Mains.
              Yours of the 3rd instant

    Will you kindly suggest an appointment to our Engineer

Mr Tempest London Bridge. I am writing him to prepare him for

your communication.

                   Yours truly.

SOUTHERN RAILWAY

894 Ex.
1436

South Eastern & Chatham Railway, **SECTION**

Telephone No.:
NEW CROSS 1256.

District Engineer's Office,

New Cross Station, S.E.14.

Refer hereto in your reply:

J/49.

RECD H.O.
4 JAN 1923
No. 7 To

4 JAN 1923

3rd January, 1923.

PORTGARD SEAT
4 . 1 . 23

Dear Sirs,

CANNON STREET STATION - NOS. 3 & 4 PLATFORMS.

I am at the present time carrying out some repairs to Nos. 3 and 4 Platforms at Cannon Street Station, and it will be necessary for your electric cables to be temporarily removed.

I shall be glad if you will kindly arrange for this to be done as early as possible.

Yours truly,

District Engineer.

THE CITY OF LONDON ELECTRIC
LIGHTING COMPANY, LIMITED,
1, Great Winchester Street,
L O N D O N,   E. C. 2.

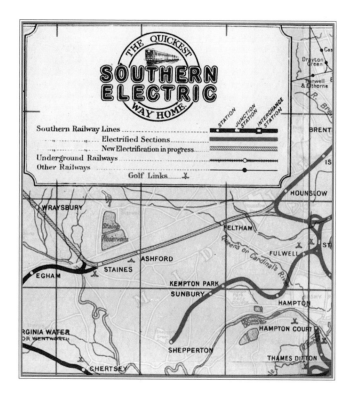

Extracts from the SR map of 1929, showing the modernistic style of artwork and an enticement to commute from the country. In those days London was much smaller, of course – Dartford and Bromley were in Kent while Croydon and Sutton were in Surrey.

TO PARIS			FROM PARIS	
P.M.				P.M.
1* 0	dep.	LONDON(Victoria)	arr.	6*45
2*38	arr.	Folkestone Harbour		
3*10	dep.			
		Dover Marine	dep.	5*13
			arr.	4*40
4*40	arr. (Br.T.)	Calais Maritime	(Br.T.) dep.	3*20
5 40	arr. (F.T.)		(F.T.) dep.	4 20
6 2	dep.		arr.	4 5
9 40	arr.	PARIS(Nord)	dep.	12 45

*—One hour later until 4 October, 1958, and from 19 April, 1959.
Br.T.—British Time.
F.T.—French Time(coincides with British Time until 4 October, 1958, and from 19 April, 1959; one hour in advance of British Time from 5 October, 1958, to 18 April, 1959).

FARES

LONDON TO PARIS (including supplement for reservation of Pullman seats on both sides of the Channel).

	1st Class (available 2 months)
SINGLE	£8 . 7 . 0
RETURN	£16 14 . 0

The fares quoted above are liable to alteration.

Extracts from a BR(S) 'Golden Arrow' leaflet of 1958, showing the chic design of the cover, also the train times and fares (which included meals). Exactly forty years later, in mid-1998, the equivalent journey by 'Eurostar' from Waterloo to Paris (Nord) takes four hours and costs £305 for a two-month first-class return (with no meals), or £159 for a three-day weekend first-class return.

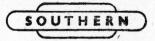

SOUTHERN

GOOD FRIDAY, EASTER SUNDAY & MONDAY
APRIL 15th, 17th & 18th
EXCURSIONS
To Allhallows-on-Sea

FROM	DEPART Friday and Sunday a.m.	a.m.	a.m.	p.m.	DEPART Monday a.m.	a.m.	a.m.	a.m.	p.m.	Return Fares, 2nd Class
	7 49	9 59	10 59	12 39	7 49	9 59	10 59	11 59	12 39	s. d.
CHARING CROSS	7 49	9 59	10 59	12 39	7 49	9 59	10 59	11 59	12 39	
WATERLOO	7 51	10 1	11 1	12 41	7 51	10 1	11 1	12 1 p.m.	12 41	7/6
LONDON BRIDGE	7 56	10 6	11 6	12 46	7 56	10 6	11 6	12 6	12 46	
DEPTFORD	7B 56	9 B 56	10B 56	12B 26	7B 56	9B 56	10B 56	11B 56 a.m.	12B 26	7/-
GREENWICH	7B 58	9 B 56	10B 58	12B 28	7B 58	9B 58	10B 58	11B 58	12B 28	
MAZE HILL	8B 1	10B 1	11B 1	12B 31	8B 1	10B 1	11B 1	12B 1 p.m.	12B 31	6/6
WESTCOMBE PARK	8B 3	10B 3	11B 3	12B 33	8B 3	10B 3	11B 3	12B 3	12B 33	
NEW CROSS	8 1	10 11	11 11	12 51	8 1	10 11	11 11	12 11	12 51	7/-
ST. JOHNS	8 4	10 14	11 14	12 54	8 4	10 14	11 14	12 14	12 54	
LEWISHAM	8 6	10 16	11 16	12 56	8 6	10 16	11 16	12 16	12 56	
BLACK HEATH	8 8	10 18	11 18	12 58	8 8	10 18	11 18	12 18	12 58	6/6
CHARLTON	8B 6	10B 6	11B 6	12B 36	8B 6	10B 6	11B 6	12B 6	12B 36	
WOOLWICH DOCKYARD	8B 8	10B 8	11B 8	12B 38	8B 8	10B 8	11B 8	12B 8	12B 38	
WOOLWICH ARSENAL	8B 11	10B 11	11B 11	12B 41	8B 11	10B 11	11B 11	12B 11	12B 41	6/-
PLUMSTEAD	8B 13	10B 13	11B 13	12B 43	8B 13	10B 13	11B 13	12B 13	12B 43	
ABBEY WOOD	8B 16	10B 16	11B 16	12B 46	8B 16	10B 16	11B 16	12B 16	12B 46	
BELVEDERE	8B 19	10B 19	11B 19	12B 49	8B 19	10B 19	11B 19	12B 19	12B 49	5/6
ERITH	8B 22	10B 22	11B 22	12B 52	8B 22	10B 22	11B 22	12B 22	12B 52	5/-
KIDBROOKE	8 11	10 21	11 21	1 1	8 11	10 21	11 21	12 21	1 1	6/6
ELTHAM (Well Hall)	8 14	10 24	11 24	1 4	8 14	10 24	11 24	12 24	1 4	
ELTHAM PARK	8 16	10 26	11 26	1 6	8 16	10 26	11 26	12 26	1 6	6/-
FALCONWOOD	8 18	10 28	11 28	1 8	8 18	10 28	11 28	12 28	1 8	
WELLING	8 21	10 31	11 31	1 11	8 21	10 31	11 31	12 31	1 11	
BEXLEYHEATH	8 24	10 34	11 34	1 14	8 24	10 34	11 34	12 34	1 14	5/6
BARNEHURST	8 27	10 37	11 37	1 17	8 27	10 37	11 37	12 37	1 17	5/-
HITHER GREEN	7B 58	10B 5	11B 7	12B 45	7B 58	10B 5	11B 5	12B 5	12B 45	6/6
LEE	8B 0	10B 7	11B 7	12B 47	8B 0	10B 7	11B 7	12B 7	12B 47	
MOTTINGHAM	8B 3	10B 10	11B 10	12B 50	8B 3	10B 10	11B 10	12B 10	12B 50	6/-
NEW ELTHAM	8B 6	10B 13	11B 13	12B 53	8B 6	10B 13	11B 13	12B 13	12B 53	
SIDCUP	8B 9	10B 16	11B 16	12B 56	8B 9	10B 16	11B 16	12B 16	12B 56	5/6
ALBANY PARK	8B 12	10B 19	11B 19	12B 59	8B 12	10B 19	11B 19	12B 19	12B 59	
BEXLEY	8B 15	10B 22	11B 22	1B 2	8B 15	10B 22	11B 22	12B 22	1B 2	5/-
CRAYFORD	8B 18	10B 25	11B 25	1B 5	8B 18	10B 25	11B 25	12B 25	1B 5	
SLADE GREEN	8B 25	10B 25	11B 25	12B 55	8B 25	10B 25	11B 25	12B 25	12B 55	5/-
DARTFORD	8 33	10 43	11 43	1 23	8 33	10 43	11 43	12 43	1 23	4/6
STONE CROSSING HALT	8 37	10 47	11 47	1 27	8 37	10 47	11 47	12 47	1 27	
GREENHITHE	8 39	10 49	11 49	1 29	8 39	10 49	11 49	12 49	1 29	4/-
SWANSCOMBE HALT	8 42	10 52	11 52	1 32	8 42	10 52	11 52	12 52	1 32	
NORTHFLEET	8 45	10 55	11 55	1 35	8 45	10 55	11 55	12 55	1 35	3/6
GRAVESEND CENTRAL	8 54	11 5	12 5 p.m.	1 54	8 58	11 5	12 5 p.m.	1 5	1 54	2/-
CLIFFE	9 7	11 18	12 17	2 7	9 11	11 18	12 17	1 24	2 7	
Allhallows .. arrive	9 28	11 39	12 35	2 28	9 34	11 39	12 35	1 42	2 28	

B—Change at Dartford.

→ **RETURN BY ANY TRAIN, SAME DAY** ←

Passengers should ascertain if (and where) change of carriage is necessary

CHILDREN 3 AND UNDER 14 YEARS, HALF FARE

Tickets may be obtained in advance at Booking Stations or Travel Agencies

QUICKER ON THE JOURNEY — LONGER BY THE SEA

> **For your Summer Holidays. Don't forget that if you can travel mid-week British Railways offer you a 25% reduction on fares for journeys over 100 miles**

61 Queen Street, E.C.4.
February, 1960   S.E.30/A15⁄29260   (S)   Printed in Great Britain by C.M.D. Printers Ltd., London and Chatham.

INDEX OF PHOTOGRAPHIC LOCATIONS